Soccer Illustrated

Soccer
Illustrated

by Frank F. DiClemente

Coach of Soccer, Phillips Academy,
Andover, Mass.

Illustrated by William Abbott Cheever

A. S. BARNES AND COMPANY *New York*

Contents

v

Illustrations and Diagrams

DIAGRAMS

Soccer Illustrated

O—OFFENSIVE PLAYER

X—DEFENSIVE PLAYER

_____ —DIRECTION OF PLAYER

∿∿∿—DRIBBLE

- - - - - -—FLIGHT OF BALL

ⓧ— BALL

CF—*Center Forward*

I—*Inside*

LI—*Left Inside*

RI—*Right Inside*

WF—*Wing Forward*

LW—*Left Wing*

RW—*Right Wing*

CH—*Center Halfback*

WH—*Wing Halfback*

ʅ **LH**—*Left Halfback*

ɣ **RH**—*Right Halfback*

FB—*Fullback*

ʅ **LFB**—*Left Fullback*

ʋ **RFB**—*Right Fullback*

╎ **G**—*Goalie*

FIGURE I   LEGEND

I

Introduction

Several lives lost by drowning." These words in a news-
paper account of an athletic contest would certainly be reason
enough for exclamation in this day and age. However, long ago,
that and many similar oddities were the reasons for the game of
soccer's being outlawed in England because it was considered "a
bloodie and murthering practice rather than a fellowly sport or
pastime." Soccer was referred to as a "friendlie kind of fighting!"
Goals two miles apart; games played in streets from one end of
town to the other; balls lodged in gutters and rooftops; several
hundreds of people taking part, with the game lasting all day
and into the night—such details give one a reasonably good idea
about the evolution of this game of soccer. Its development was
slow, considering that it was introduced in England in some form
when the Romans invaded the country, and that it wasn't until
around 1860 that an organization was formed and a consolida-
tion of the rules was begun.

The progress in any game can be followed by the changes made in the rules. Some of the more important milestones of the game during its growing stages in England were:

1867—First crossbar on goal nine feet from ground, first marking of field, first mention of corner kick, first mention of goal to be scored directly from free kick; players defending against a free kick less than six yards from goal did not have to stand behind goal line.

1870—Charging from behind was prohibited.

1871—Goalie was first allowed to use hands.

1874-75—The old plan of changing ends after each score was changed to the present rule—a crossbar on the goal was accepted as an option for the tape.

1878-79—Added to the laws of the game was: No player shall charge his opponent by leaping at him.

1880—Referee was first mentioned in the regulations.

1881-82—New law giving official the power to allow a goal when the ball had been handled by a player other than the goalkeeper if in the official's opinion the ball would have passed between the posts—nature of an experiment.

1882—Size of ball was standardized and use of tape across the top of goal was tossed out in favor of crossbar—charging from behind was modified—heretofore out altogether.

1883-84—Previously there were six forwards, two halfbacks, two fullbacks, one goalie. At this time the third half was introduced, taking one of the forwards off the front line, that is, the duplicate center forward.

1885—It was first realized that the two fulls and the goalies should work as a unit. Up to this time combinations were only thought of on attack.

1887—New rule stated that a ball that went beyond an imaginary touch line while in the air was out of bounds—heretofore it was in play if it landed back on the field of play—throw-up to restart the game was put into the rules.

1888-89—The referee was given more powers, including that of giving free kicks for foul play without waiting for an appeal.

1890–91—"Penalty kick" was introduced—helped refs check practice of stopping a goal being scored at any cost. At this point also the linesmen replaced the umpires who up to this time were almost a hindrance to the referee. The linesman's duties were to declare when the ball went over the touch line —thus the referee became the autocrat.

1891—The use of goal nets was first introduced in 1891, an innovation which has proved to be one of the most valuable aids to the referee that could have been designed.

1902—At the annual meeting of the Association a motion was passed prohibiting the referee, linesman or players from making any bets.

Although soccer has been played in colleges in the United States as early as 1860, it has been very slow in capturing the imagination of the American spectator. It might come as a surprise to the American public to learn that soccer is played in more countries in the world than any other game, and it draws more spectators each year than any other game. In the last ten years soccer has grown more in stature than in the combined ninety-five years of its existence in the United States. The most important contributing factor is that more young career men in the field of athletics, who know and love the game because of actually playing it, are coaching and working on committees in the promotion of the sport. In the past, bless 'em all, the fortunes of the game have been in the hands of men who coached on a part-time basis, and who had little or no time to devote to its general promotion outside of their immediate locality. Soccer is destined to be the most widely played game in the States before too long. My only hope is that the powers to be don't explore its potential as a source of revenue. In substance, there is no basis for this, since the cost to schools and the players alike is very small. Soccer has every requisite to appeal to large numbers of players and spectators and take its place alongside other sports in this respect. The game has sustained action with very few or no interruptions, and its basic patterns are simple and easily understood. Both the individual and combination play can be spectacular enough to keep any group on the edge of their seats. For soccer to take its place alongside baseball, football, basketball and other sports in spectator and player appeal here in the States, the quality and the standards of the game must be exceedingly high. It is hoped that this book, in some small way, will help in establishing these necessary higher standards of play.

Rather than go into detail regarding the progress of soccer in the States, I refer the reader to Mr. Frank G. Menke's book, "The Encyclopedia of Sports," published by A. S. Barnes, which contains a very thorough history of soccer in the United States.

Soccer is a game, and as far back as I can remember, games have meant fun, relaxation, satisfaction and friends. When a player fails to derive these simple feelings, then, to him it should no longer be a game. Games teach us that there is more fun and satisfaction in winning than losing, and a player should always play to win.

Soccer can be played by boys of all ages and all sizes, and it offers each player the satisfaction of playing individually and together with other boys. Soccer is a game of limited and controlled bodily contact, but enough to fire a boy with the great desire to be better than those he is playing against. If, through playing, this all-important desire of wanting to be better, wanting to win, and wanting to do his best is aroused in the player, then the game is worth while. Soccer does this. Soccer is a game that can be adapted to either sex, and regardless of how vigorously it is played, the chances of injury are very small. It is a game that demands a good deal of running, which in itself is the simplest and safest exercise possible for the development of any boy or girl. It is a game that does not demand brute strength or great size as a requisite. It is a game that can be played as an organized part of any program with very little expense to the boy or to the school.

Soccer, like all other games, is played according to principles, and winners are determined by how much knowledge of the prin-

ciples the players have, and the extent to which they put this
knowledge to use. The purpose of this book will be accomplished
if it gives the readers the knowledge, the methods, and the desire
to put these principles to use to their greatest advantage and with
the least amount of effort.

Knowledge of the principles, per se, does not stamp a player for
ultimate success. He must present some natural ability, and some
spark must kindle his enthusiasm and love for the game so that he
is willing to sacrifice and work to become adept in the use of this
knowledge. The brunt of kindling this spark falls on the shoulders
of the coach. For the coach to be able to do this, he should know
his subject, he should know how to teach it, and he must be vigorously enthusiastic about it. It is hoped that this book will stimulate the imaginations of all coaches so that they may develop new
approaches in presenting new and original material to the boys,
thereby creating new-found enthusiasm, better players and better teams.

No matter how successful a coach has been he should never
feel that his way is the only way, and that he knows all there is
to know about the sport. A wise coach will be a tolerant and a
very attentive listener. He must realize that the more ways he
knows of doing things the more interesting and enthusiastic re-
sponse he will get from the squad.

The coach can and must set the tone of the practice sessions,
establish the outlook and purpose of the team, and through constant planning come up with new, sound and original ideas. Originality puts spice, dash, freshness and appeal into a program. The
coach is responsible for keeping interest high and practices well
organized. He must make his boys feel that, if the game is worth
while, it is worth playing well; irresponsible, indifferent and hap-
hazard spirit should not be condoned.

The coach must realize that the boys on the squad have vary-
ing degrees of natural ability, different temperaments and person-
alities, and that his job is to bring out the most and the best of
each. The coach must be able to get the most out of every mem-

ber of his squad by knowing, through experience and study, how each man responds to flattery, riding, bullying, sympathy and understanding. He must exert authority without seeming to. He must demand respect by what he knows and does. He must breed confidence in his players by being sure that what he is teaching them is sound. He must have the knack of spotting potential in a boy, and of knowing how to bring each one along at the right pace so that, when he calls on him, he is ready. He must be able to place a boy in the position to which he is best suited, and then have him specialize so that he can develop the tricks that will make him brilliant individually and in combination. This brilliance will come if the coach, by encouraging initiative, leads the boy into developing his own style. Although there are certain rules of thumb for every position, the more original a player can be, the more effective he will be.

The coach must be able to keep the boys all fighting for the same end, and develop team spirit and a strong friendly feeling among them. He must teach the boys the value of clean play and encourage them to set their standards high.

Through the coach the boys learn that, even in a loss, something can be salvaged by analyzing their play, finding out why they lost, and then setting out to correct their weaknesses by hard work. The coach must be able to spot weaknesses and handle the boys in such a way that they will work vigorously to correct them on their own initiative. In some cases, perhaps, the coach should wisely and subtly work out a program to correct a player's weaknesses.

The spark of enthusiasm can also be aroused in young players by watching outstanding players perform, and by having more experienced and highly successful members of the squad take a humble and sincere interest in the welfare of the beginners.

The game of soccer brings out and develops many fine qualities in a boy. It is a game which, when played right, demands high standards of physical and mental alertness. It demands and develops stamina, co-ordination, agility, speed, courage, determination, initiative, resourcefulness and many other basic qualities. Every situation offers a boy a chance to develop originality and keen judgment. Every move in soccer, once it "gets in a boy's blood," will be sheer pleasure and delight. A boy will learn to sacrifice, to blend his individual ability into wise and effective combination play with his teammates. He will learn that when he steps on the field he has a job to do, and with good coaching and diligent practice he will know how to best go about it. He will learn to adapt himself so as to make the most of any situation that presents itself. He learns never to quit. Instead he calls on every bit of strength, when the pressure is on, and usually meets the challenge.

He must learn to use what ability he has to his team's advantage and make the most use of it. What he lacks in size he must make up for in courage, clever ball handling and subtle combination play.

He must learn all the fundamentals and practice earnestly to execute them with intelligence and purpose, fairly and effectively. His movements should never be aimless and without purpose. He should be using his head as well as his body at all times. A player who is going to outwit the opponents must have more than one trick up his sleeve and should always be working to develop them. A boy can benefit a great deal through participating in soccer, but he will only get out of it what he puts into it.

II

Equipment

THE FIELD AND PRACTICE EQUIPMENT

IN CONSTRUCTING a soccer field it is well to consider all problems and eliminate as many as possible before any actual work is done. If it is a question of money, beg, borrow, or steal it, but do the job right when it is being done—it will be money in the bank and will save much time and many headaches in the long run. In laying out the field some of the factors to consider are:

The Size of the Field

The rule book states that the maximum width of a soccer field should be 75 yards and the minimum width 65 yards; the maximum length 120 yards and the minimum length 110 yards. However, the age of the group for whom the field is being constructed should determine its size.

Grade of Field

The field should have a slope of about two or three inches for every 100 feet. This is for drainage purposes.

8

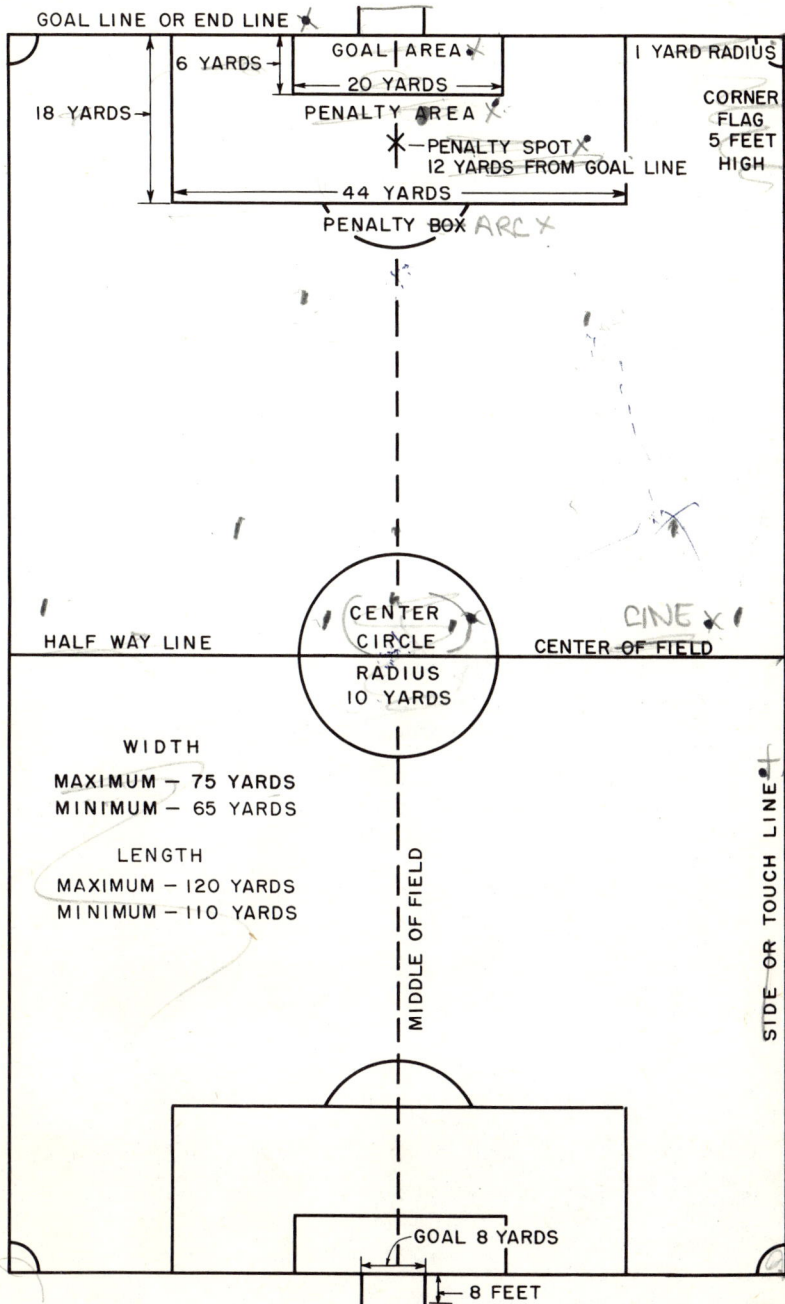

GOAL LINE OR END LINE

1 YARD RADIUS

GOAL AREA

6 YARDS

20 YARDS

CORNER
FLAG
5 FEET
HIGH

18 YARDS

PENALTY AREA

PENALTY SPOT
12 YARDS FROM GOAL LINE

44 YARDS

PENALTY BOX ARC

CENTER
CIRCLE
RADIUS
10 YARDS

HALF WAY LINE

LINE

CENTER OF FIELD

WIDTH

MAXIMUM — 75 YARDS
MINIMUM — 65 YARDS

LENGTH

MAXIMUM — 120 YARDS
MINIMUM — 110 YARDS

MIDDLE OF FIELD

SIDE OR TOUCH LINE

GOAL 8 YARDS

8 FEET

DIAGRAM I

THE FIELD—ITS DIMENSIONS
AND MARKINGS

Topsoil

Every consideration should be given in getting a topsoil that will eliminate all possibilities of the field pulling apart with use. Holes and grass not well rooted can often cause serious ankle and leg injuries.

About three to four inches of loam, sown with tough grass having strong roots, is most desirable. The use of the following grass-seed mixture has proven very successful: 50 per cent Kentucky Blue, 25 per cent Creeping Red Fescue, 5 per cent Colonial Bent, 10 per cent Red Top, 10 per cent Domestic Rye Grass.

The following is the best procedure in putting the top dressing on the field:

1. Cover field with a three- to four-inch top dressing of loam.
2. Rake field down three inches to remove stones.
3. Roll field.
4. Brush field with a steel matting or a long plank with brush (limbs of trees) attached. The long plank will level off high spots and fill in holes, and the brush will smooth off field.
5. Land lime the field—a powdered dry lime. The topsoil should have a Ph of between 6.5 and 7.5.
6. Brush lime in.
7. Seed field with suggested grass mixture—brush in.
8. Roll lightly. (At this stage light showers will help.)
9. When grass is up three inches, give it a light rolling.
10. A few days later fix cutters on mower to cut grass to two inches in height.

Position of Sun During Practice Sessions and at Game Time

Most sun problems will be eliminated if the field is laid out lengthwise from north to south.

Drainage

Base should afford good drainage. If the base is gravel, a clay binder should be mixed in to avoid a drainage that is too fast, and hence a hard field. It is wise to provide good drainage to about one foot below the surface. This will make for a nice springy topsoil and optimum conditions for strong-rooted grass to take hold.

Nearness of Field to Dressing Room
Comfortable Between-the-Periods Accommodations
Available Ground Around Field

Around the field it is wise to have as much usable ground as possible for spectator room and for equipment. Any equipment which will help in the development of fundamentals should be set up and made available adjacent to the field. A rebound or kick board is very valuable in learning and practicing. This is constructed of wood and usually larger than the size of the mouth of the goal. The outline of a goal can be painted on the board with various targets positioned to help in developing accuracy in the use of the fundamentals. The advantage of a rebound board is that a player can, by himself, practice kicking, trapping, heading and passing with little or no wasted time. The targets will offer the players enough satisfaction to sustain interest.

Dribbling can be practiced with the use of permanent stakes placed in a straight line at various distances from each other. There are many other pieces of original equipment that have been used in developing fundamentals. They should all be simple so that it doesn't take a big staff to put them up, take them down, or replace them.

The field should be rolled, but not more than twice a week during the season, and the grass should be kept to about two or three inches in height. To keep the field in good shape, it should be seeded early in the spring. With the seeding a good commercial fertilizer, such as 8–6–4, should be used, that is, 8 parts nitrogen, 6 parts phosphorus and 4 parts potash. Occasionally lime should be used to sweeten the soil. Some schools have been bothered with the Japanese beetle which does a good deal of damage to the soil. To combat this, mix chlordane with water and wet down the field. Wetting down the field with arsenate of lead will also help in combating the Japanese beetle.

To mark the field it is best to first use hot wet lime, which will burn the markings in; thereafter, hydrated lime should be used. In wet weather some schools have found dry powdered lime most practical.

PLAYERS' AND GAME EQUIPMENT

There is a good deal of truth in the saying that you play as you look. Clothes never yet made a man, but they certainly make a terrific impression and can have a great psychological effect on a man's behavior. Good athletes will usually be very conscious of the condition and appearance of their equipment. Practice clothing should be clean and warm, especially where players must contend with sharp, cold fall winds. It is wise to have a jersey with some wool or flannel in it for the wet and cold days. On the hot Indian summer days it is best to wear a light T shirt type of cotton jersey. Heavy, uncomfortable jerseys on hot days will sap the strength of the best-conditioned athlete, to say nothing about the poorly conditioned ones.

Pants should be loose with plenty of room for the legs to move freely. A boxer type short seems to be the most comfortable. All equipment should give the wearer freedom of movement.

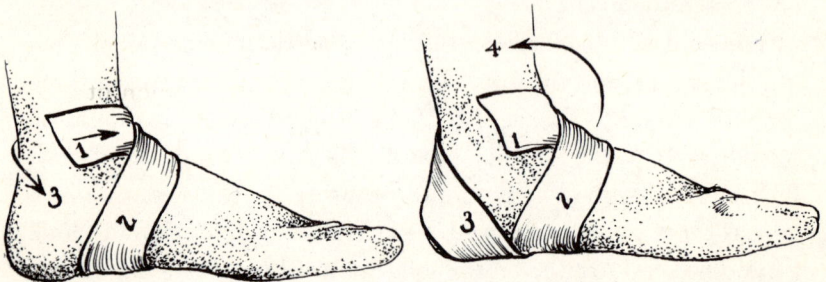

ILLUSTRATION I   PUTTING ON AN ANKLE WRAP

Blisters raise havoc with many teams, and players are often lost to a team because of them. One way to avoid this is to wear two pairs of socks, one cotton next to the skin, and one wool over the cotton. Many teams successfully use skin hardeners, such as tincture of benzoin. For the good of the team none of these methods of preventing blisters should be taken lightly. Many boys think that shin pads are worn only by the less manly, that they show lack of courage. All coaches should insist on every boy wearing shin pads, regardless of make or style, as long as they fit well and feel comfortable.

Ankle wraps should be considered, the same as shin pads, a regular part of the issued equipment. A wise coach will have the trainer teach each player how to put on his own ankle wraps. The following diagram will show how to put the ankle wraps on to give the boy the greatest amount of protection and comfort. Ankle wraps can be bought in large rolls and cut to the proper lengths. Seventy-two inches seems to be the standard comfortable length for high school and prep school boys. Ninety-six inches seems to be the comfortable standard length for college players. An ankle wrap too long might prove to be bulky, uncomfortable and harmful. Clean ankle wraps and rollers should be available at all times.

There is a great divergence of opinion regarding the best soccer shoe. However, this is a personal matter, and the choice should be left entirely up to the individual. No matter what type

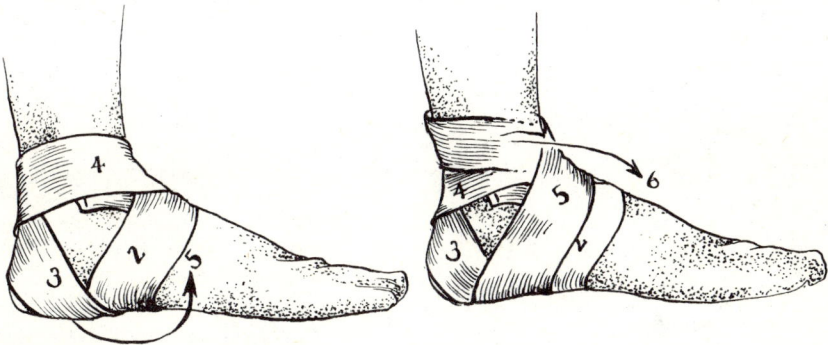

ILLUSTRATION I, CONTINUED

of shoe is used, it is wise to be sure that no cleats, nails or pegs are sticking out. It must be each player's obligation to inspect his shoes for nails or pegs sticking out. Very serious accidents have resulted through negligence. It can and should be avoided. Shoes should be oiled occasionally. When wet, they should first be dried at normal room temperatures and then oiled.

Any good leather ball can be used. The important point is that before practice each day balls should be inflated to the proper air pressure. It is wise after each game to throw the game ball into the practice bag. Practicing with a good ball will afford the players a chance of playing with a ball as near to the type used in the game as possible. Playing with a new ball, as against playing with an old one, makes a good deal of difference in the actual handling of the ball, hence, the control of the ball. Wet balls should be dried out at normal room temperatures and treated with a good leather oil.

On the off season all the equipment should be cleaned, repaired and properly stored. All balls should be stored in a room with good circulation and a temperature of not more than sixty-five to seventy degrees. Balls should be oiled before storing and inflated to half their regular air pressure.

III

Fundamentals

Soccer is a game of ball control both individually and in combination with other members of the team. To be able to control a soccer ball a player must master the fundamentals by using any part of his body but his hands and arms. The fundamentals are: kicking, passing, dribbling, trapping, tackling and heading. To master the fundamentals, a player must first know the mechanics of each and then practice them as often and as diligently as he can. To be able to do anything with the ball, a player must first get the feel of it. A player should practice the fundamentals until he can control the ball with his feet, head and body as well as a basketball player can handle a basketball with his hands. All available equipment should be used in mastering fundamentals, such as a kick board to develop kicking and passing, barrels to develop accuracy, and stakes to help improve dribbling.

It is a great source of satisfaction to a coach and to the players themselves to see eleven men well drilled in fundamentals work together as a unit. Soccer is a team game, but it also gives an individual ample opportunity to display his talents. Properly organ-

15

ILLUSTRATION 2   GENERAL INSTEP KICK

Eyes on ball—head down.

Grounded foot placed a comfortable distance to side with arch opposite the middle of ball.

Kicking leg starts back as non-kicking foot is jumping into position.

Forward motion of the kicking leg starts at hip. When the knee is over the ball the lower leg is snapped forward and at impact eye and knee are directly over foot.

Toe is pointed down and inward. The ball is hit by contact with the ball on the lace of the shoe (instep).

Immediately after impact the kicker follows through with the kicking toe still down, eyes and head still down, body begins to lean back, left leg (grounded leg of right-footed kicker) begins to straighten out, heel of left foot comes off ground followed by toe and a hop. This follow-through is very important since it will give added power to the kick.

Arms are out to sides for balance.

The ball is kicked at juncture of horizontal and vertical axis.

The placing of the grounded foot has everything to do with the loft of the kick. The ball will go in the direction the foot is pointed at the end of the follow-through.

ized team play does not oppose the individual role. Bear in mind that a properly organized team has a definite, well-planned way of advancing the ball into the scoring area. A planned attack calls for long training on fundamentals combined with the sound use of offensive plays and passing maneuvers.

This chapter is devoted to the explanation of, the use of, and the analysis of the fundamentals. If the reader does not get any more out of this material than the realization that ball control means team success, then it will have served its purpose. Ball control simply means the ability to execute fundamentals.

KICKING

In learning to kick, the reader must realize that it isn't how high or how far you kick the ball, but where you kick it that is important. Every kick should be in substance a pass. In answer to the question as to how high you should kick the ball, the for-

ILLUSTRATION 2, CONTINUED

wards and halfbacks should remember that the crossbar of a goal is eight feet above the ground and anything over that will never get into the goal. In learning to kick, some boys find the side approach, or an angle approach, to the ball much more to their liking than coming straight onto it. This does give some individuals a freer swing of the leg and it feels much more comfortable. It is, however, a matter of individual preference, and while learning, it will pay to work on this detail until the approach best suited for the individual is derived.

A good deal of practice is involved in mastering proper timing so that all the power of the leg and body are behind the kick at the moment of impact. It should be remembered that the grounded foot should stay on the ground until after the impact and then leave the ground to get the last ounce of power into the kick on the follow-through. In learning to kick, the beginner must go through the motions very slowly and objectively so as to first stress form, and then progress for accuracy, speed and distance in that order. The ball will always go in the direction the foot is pointed at the end of the follow-through if it is kicked on the vertical axis.* To learn properly and not develop any bad habits, first kick at a stationary ball.

The kicker should learn to survey the field and decide then and there where he is going to kick the ball. He then gets his eye on the ball and concentrates on putting it where—he decided a second before—it will do his team the most good.

It is generally accepted that to kick with the instep, as opposed to kicking with the toe, is much better since it will give the kicker more control of the ball. The instep should not be confused with the inside of the foot. The instep is located along the lace of the shoe. Check Illustration 2. In kicking the ball with the instep, the player should point his toe down, pigeon-toed and relaxed. The theory of the instep kick is rightly based on the assumption that the more of the foot the player has on the ball, the more control

---

* The asterisk here and throughout the text refers the reader to the Glossary at the back of the book for a full explanation of the term so marked.

ILLUSTRATION 3   VOLLEY KICK

Eyes on ball.

With the ball coming directly at the kicker, the grounded foot is bent and is placed to one side and enough in front of the oncoming ball so that when contact is made with the kicking foot, the knee of the kicking leg is slightly behind the kicking foot. The body is leaning slightly backward and the head is behind the knee rather than directly over the knee as in the general kick, that is, kicking a ball on the ground. The further back the body is leaning the higher the loft to the ball. The higher in the air the impact the higher in the air the flight of the ball. In using this kick as a clearance kick, which it is used mostly for, especially by the fullbacks, the kicker should develop the knack of getting only the amount of loft necessary by keeping these principles in mind.

The impact should be so timed that the ball is hit just as the leg is starting the upswing. The higher the impact the less power forward; all the power then is spent in sending the ball high in the air.

Keep the toe pointed and down. This is definitely an instep kick. Use arms to add power and balance. Arms out to sides in position most natural for the kicker to get most power and better balance. After impact the follow-through is the same as in the general kick.

ILLUSTRATION 4   HALF-VOLLEY KICK

A ball kicked just as it leaves the ground. It will give the kicker a long low drive. The mechanics of this kick are the same as the general kick with body well over ball. This will give the kicker a hard, low drive very effective for using in shooting directly at the goal.

ILLUSTRATION 5   PIVOT KICK

Eye on the ball; grounded foot placed to side of the oncoming ball at a com-

fortable distance and not more than twenty inches in front of it. Otherwise, power will be lost in reaching for the ball. The body should be leaning slightly back and to the side the ball is going to be kicked. The ball should be hit out in front. It is impossible to pivot kick with power and accuracy when the kicker's body is over the ball. The action of the kicking leg is from the hip. It is a sweeping circular motion with the foot hitting the ball at the vertical axis in the desired direction of the flight of the ball.

The ball should be hit with the instep with toe pointed down pigeon-toe fashion. At the finish of the follow-through the foot should be pointing in the direction the ball is aimed. The body should be leaning slightly backward and facing in the direction the ball is kicked. The pivot is made on the grounded foot.

he will have over it. More control is the big advantage the in-step kick has over the toe kick on a moving ball.

On the other hand, as much distance and control can be realized from a toe kick of a stationary ball as can be realized from that of an instep kick. On a stationary kick, such as a goal kick, some players prefer the toe kick to the instep kick. This is an individual matter. Regardless, however, of whether the toe or the instep is used, the eye must always be kept on the ball from start to finish.

The mechanics of kicking a moving ball are exactly the same as in kicking a stationary ball except for the placing of the grounded foot. In kicking a ball on the ground, rolling away from the kicker, the grounded foot must be placed to the side and in advance of the ball so that on impact the kicker's eyes, knee and foot are in a vertical perpendicular line and the ball will be opposite the instep of the grounded foot. In kicking a moving ball on the ground, rolling toward the kicker, the grounded foot is placed to the side and far enough ahead of the ball so that on impact the rolling ball will be just opposite the instep of the grounded foot.

Volley kick is mostly used by fullbacks. A clearance volley kick is usually used to clear an opponent who is driving in on the kicker. It is a first-time kick, that is, a kick that has to be made without first trapping the ball. The ball comes at the kicker on the fly or on a high bounce. The kick has to be made hurriedly and should be practiced under those conditions in an effort to develop reasonable accuracy. As a clearance kick it requires more height, since it usually has to go over the head and body of an onrushing opponent.

PASSING

Passing in soccer is the cohesion factor which molds the individual brilliance of all team members into an effective team machine. Passing is the link between players that develops team spirit and holds a team together. One good pass at the right time

ILLUSTRATION 6   PUSH PASS WITH INSIDE OF FOOT

The approach should be timed so that on impact the grounded foot is close, to the side, and slightly behind the ball. If the ball is moving toward or away from the kicker, the foot is placed so that when impact is made the grounded foot will be slightly behind and to the side of the ball. If the grounded foot is too far forward and too close along side of the ball on impact, accuracy and range of passing will be diminished.

On kicking, the shoulders and hips turn slightly away from the ball while raising the kicking leg, which should be bent slightly at the knee, with the knee and foot turned slightly outward. The body should be well over the ball at the time of impact. The foot should be only slightly off the ground on impact (kicking foot), head down and eyes on ball.

To hit the ball with the inside of the foot the kicker should make an easy sweeping movement of the leg from the hip, following through after impact. During the kick and follow-through, the inside of the foot should be facing in the desired direction of the pass.

A push pass is a short pass and should always be made on the ground. It is the most accurate of all passes.

INSIDE-OF-THE-FOOT LOB PASS

Eye on ball.

Body should be oblique to the oncoming ball, that is, body should not be facing ball head on.

Kicking foot gets in position by raising leg as in taking a step up.

Obviously the inside of the kicking foot is facing the oncoming ball.

The ball is hit with the inside of the foot. The higher off the ground the ball is met the higher in the air the ball will go.

from one teammate to another can do more to develop team morale and spirit than reams and reams of words. Passing, of course, like other things, can be overdone and should not be indulged in simply for the sake of doing it. Passing should be used intelligently and with a purpose. It is the basis for successful team play, and most of the time the easiest and quickest way to get the ball to the goal.

All kicks should be considered passes, and every effort should be made to kick accurately to an open space or to an open man. To be able to make every kick a pass, the kicker must have a reasonable mental picture of the positions of each man on the field. Only keeping alert and constantly studying positions of opponents and

The body with the start of the kicking motion begins to lean in the opposite direction of the motion of the kicking leg for balance and power. The power comes from the knee.

at which the inside of the foot hits the ball.

This pass is used to clear the ball over the head of an opponent. It can be either a ball played as it comes in on the fly or on the bounce.

teammates will turn a wild aimless kicking game into a smooth, beautiful passing attack.

Horse sense tells us that a job shared by eleven men is more apt to achieve its ultimate objective than a job done by one. Passing offers opportunity for the team to share the load. Passing means combination play where two or more men team up to get the ball to the goal in the fastest way and with the minimum amount of effort. When the situation presents itself, it is much easier and offers many more opportunities to draw a man and pass off than to dribble by or around a man. Check Diagram 21; page 140. A rule of thumb for the passer is always to move into position for a repass after passing off. Intelligent positioning of a player without the ball leads to many opportunities.

The long pass (either to a spot or to an open teammate) can be

ILLUSTRATION 8   SOLE-OF-THE-FOOT PASS

It is done merely by putting the sole of the foot lightly on the ball and literally pulling it backwards. This pass can be used for change of direction while dribbling, or it can be used as a short pass. It can be a very deceptive maneuver.

used in placing the ball quickly behind the defense. It can be an accurate clearing* kick to a spot, usually for the wing forwards or center forward; or a cross from a wing halfback to the opposite wing forward; or a pass from wing forward to wing forward. However, no matter which pass pattern is used, the point behind all long passes is to get down the field behind the defense to the mouth of the goal with as few kicks as necessary, in the quickest way with the most men, so as to give the offensive team the most and the best opportunities.

The effect of an accurate long cross or pass to the opposite side of the field explains the rule of thumb: always pass in the direction opposite to that in which you are moving. In substance, it means that the strength of the defense will be on the side of the field where the play is, and a quick cross down and to the opposite side of the field will hit the defense at their weakest spot at that particular moment.

ILLUSTRATION 9   HEELING

Heeling is kicking or passing the ball by using the heel of the foot. It is done merely by stepping over the ball and kicking backwards. It is usually a short pass and when used while dribbling can be very deceptive.

The long pass should be an instep kick. Its height, direction and speed are determined by the position of the ball on the field and the purpose of the pass. A cross pass must be one that has enough loft and speed to carry to the players on the opposite side of the field. A center or cross by the wing must be high enough to clear the defending backs, and easy and accurate enough for the forwards to handle. These passes are usually lead passes to a spot behind the defense.

Hitting a pass too hard for the receiver to handle is like kicking the ball away. A pass to a covered man is useless; on the other hand, giving the covered man a lead pass to an open spot is intelligent and effective passing. A player should learn to pass so that the receiver can get control of the ball while expending the minimum amount of effort and time. A pass to a man standing still usually ends in an interception and loss of ball. The passer

ILLUSTRATION 10   FLICK PASS

A flick pass is nothing more than a peck at the ball with the outside of the foot around the small toe for a short, deceptive pass to the side. It is usually a pass made while dribbling.

Eye on the ball.

Weight on the grounded foot which is the rear foot.

Ball is slightly out in front of the body.

Foot making pass is slightly off the ground.

The impact is made by flicking the front part of the foot out from the ankle and hitting the ball just behind the small toe on the outside of the foot. The motion is almost the same as keeping the heel on the ground and describing an arc with the toes.

Follow through with a slight outward movement at the knee and the hips. These are follow-through movements since the impetus comes from flicking the toe part of the foot outward, at the ball.

should conceal his intentions until the pass is actually made. As in all other fundamentals, passing should be practiced in all kinds of weather so that the players can learn how the ball behaves in all conditions.

Pivot kick is used mostly by the forwards, especially the wings,

ILLUSTRATION 11　　　　　INSIDE-OF-THE-FOOT DRIBBLE

Eye on ball, head and body well over ball.
Ball hit with the inside of the foot from the arch forward.
Ball tapped or pushed, not kicked, forward, always under control of the dribbler's feet. Ball tapped forward in straight line, not zigzag.
Ball is tapped forward with one foot then the other in regular running stride.

in corner kicks, centering, and in crossing the ball. The pivot kick can be made either when coming in at an angle or straight in at the ball. With practice this kick can be very deceptive. The placing of the pivot foot is all important since its position will effect the swing of the kicking foot. If the pivot foot is too close to the ball, the swing to hit the ball will be cramped and lack power and accuracy. If the pivot foot is too far away from the ball, the kicker will be reaching and lose power.

DRIBBLING

Dribbling adds to individual brilliance and can well fit into the team picture if the players know when to do it. A dribble should never take the place of a pass that can be made to an

ILLUSTRATION 12   OUTSIDE-OF-THE-FOOT DRIBBLE

Eyes on ball, head and body well over ball.
Ball is tapped forward in a straight line with outside of foot.
Foot pushing ball is turned in so that it contacts the ball near the little toe.
Running strides are not broken when the ball is pushed ahead. Distance ball is tapped forward each time is left up to the discretion of the dribbler, however, always keeping in mind that he has the ball under control.

open spot or teammate. It might be wise occasionally for a dribbler to get by one man, but to try to dribble through two or three will more than likely end in the loss of the ball. If a player does elect to dribble by an opponent and is successful, he must know what he is going to do with the ball when he gets by. A dribble can and should be used when the player does not have anyone to pass to and the logical open spots are pretty well covered. A dribble should be used to draw an opponent so as to open a teammate for a pass and a march toward the goal. The use of a dribble is justified if the dribbler has but one man to clear to get in for a shot at the goal.

Dribbling can and should be used in making the team's offense varied and effective. If used with good judgment in setting up a teammate, or in maneuvering for a good open-spot pass, or for any other reason that will keep the defense jittery and honest, then the dribble is good because it is being used as a team weapon. On the other hand, its use without any definite objective should be discouraged. Dribbling should be blended in as a part of the team and combination play.

In dribbling, the first thing that should be kept in mind is control. The last thing that should happen to the dribbler is to be tackled with the ball and lose it. The rule of thumb is to keep the ball on the toe; however, the dribbler should use his own judgment in this, since there are times when it is wiser and just as safe to push the ball ahead more than the length of a stride. Oftentimes if the forwards get the jump on the defense, a couple of long dribbles before he hits the penalty box will make the difference in getting or not getting a clean shot at the goal without breaking stride.

To get by one man, the dribbler should develop a few feints with his body, head and feet. Also he should learn to use a deceptive change of direction and pace to outsmart the tackler. In countering these moves the tackler should keep his eye on the ball or, according to some coaches, on the dribbler's hips, to avoid being faked out of position.

Once the dribbler gets by a man he should not try to outsmart the rest of the team on solo dribbling. The longer he holds onto the ball, the more time he gives the opponent's defense to get organized to stop the offensive thrust.

Fullbacks should dribble only when it is absolutely necessary. The halfbacks should pass in preference to dribbling, with one exception, that is, when the opportunity presents itself to dribble in and take a shot. The wing forwards should develop the outside-of-the-foot dribble for speed, but should be able to use the inside-of-the-foot dribble to get by one man. The inside men and center forward should use the dribble for deception, control and the preface

ILLUSTRATION 13   SOLE-OF-THE-FOOT TRAP ON
                                   ROLLING GROUND BALL

Keep eye on the ball, head down.
Get directly in front of the oncoming ball.
Proper timing is essential.
Reach out with either foot—reaching forward with the trapping foot to meet the ball.
Leg of rear or stationary foot is slightly bent at the knee.
Weight of body is borne on stationary foot.
The ball is wedged in between the foot and the ground—heel of trapping foot down, toe up—leg slightly bent.

to shots and accurate short passes; hence perfection of the inside-of-the-foot dribble with them is a must.

In dribbling too much the dribbler is apt to lose contact with the rest of the players on the field and lose the chance of a quick pass to a teammate or an open spot that may appear just before the dribble. To size up any opening while dribbling, the eye should be taken off the ball just before or after the tap and this should be done only by raising of the eyes, not the entire head.

ILLUSTRATION 14

SOLE-OF-THE-FOOT TRAP
ON BOUNCING BALL

Mechanics of this trap are the same as the rolling ball trap with the following differences: The trapping foot gives a little by bending at the knee on the impact. The foot and body are over the ball just a little more than on the rolling ball trap. It is as though the trapper is stepping lightly on the ball.

A simple fake while dribbling is to step lightly on the ball and pull it back, pivot on the grounded foot and head in the opposite direction. Check Illustration 8. Keep body between opponent and ball. Or, with a man coming in at the dribbler, the latter, instead of pushing the ball with the inside of his foot, steps over the ball and pushes it to the outside and away from the oncoming tackler with the outside of the same foot.

Of course a head, shoulder, or foot fake can be used to get by an opponent, but the beginner must first learn to keep the ball under control while dribbling. After that the time is ripe to develop the feints and fakes, but not before.

The inside-of-the-foot dribble, although not quite as fast as the outside-of-the-foot dribble, is easier to control and makes it harder for the tackler to take the ball away since it is completely engulfed by the dribbler with his body well over the ball and well protected by his legs and feet. A rule of thumb is to keep the body always between the ball and the tackler. With the inside-of-the-foot dribble there is more chance for feinting and faking and deception. Hence, this dribble should be used by the forwards and by any player aiming to get by a would-be tackler. Change of direction and pace can be made with little chance of giving away any such intention until the moves are actually made.

Although accuracy and deception *can* be developed with the use of the outside-of-the-foot dribble, the one noticeable edge the use of it has over the inside-of-the-foot dribble is speed. Of course, it can be used by any player but should be developed more by the wing forwards than any other players on the team since speed in bringing the ball down the field is so important for them.

TRAPPING

Trapping a ball means getting control of a ball that is coming at a player in the air or on the ground, from any angle or height, by the use of head, body, legs or feet. In all trapping there are a few general rules to keep in mind. First, a trap can be called successful only when the trapper gets control of the ball. The ball must be so handled that it either drops at the feet of the trapper or within a controlled distance so that the player can gather it in and make an intelligent offensive move. A ball that rebounds out of control after an attempted trap will many times give the opponent control of the ball.

The trap pass is a helpful skill which should be learned by every soccer player. It can be merely a deflection of the ball to a teammate, or can be used to deflect the ball to one side of an onrushing opponent, allowing the trapper in one motion to trap and push the ball to one side out of the reach of the onrushing opponent. The trapper, then, merely follows the ball and is on his way with the opponent behind.

In kicking a ball against a stone wall you will find it bouncing

ILLUSTRATION 15 (LEFT)   **INSIDE-OF-THE-FOOT TRAP ON BALL ROLLING ON GROUND**

Used for getting control of the ball coming from the side or an angle.

Eye on the ball.

Body leaning slightly in direction of oncoming ball ready to smother ball.

Weight is borne on foot on side ball is coming. Knee and foot bent slightly outward in the direction of oncoming ball.

Knee and foot of trapping leg are bent outward ready to smother the ball.

On impact the trapping foot is off the ground slightly and gives to cushion the effect of the impact. The inside of the foot is facing the ground slightly to wedge the ball between the foot and ground.

ILLUSTRATION 16 (RIGHT)   **INSIDE-OF-THE-FOOT TRAP ON BOUNCING BALL**

Eye on ball.

Body leaning slightly to side in direction ball is coming ready to smother ball.

Weight borne on foot nearest oncoming ball, foot and knee are bent slightly outward in the direction of the oncoming ball.

The trapping foot should be off the ground with the knee slightly out ready to smother the ball by wedging it in between the inside of the foot and the ground. Trapping foot and leg held loosely.

Timing is very essential in this since the ball should be wedged in between the side of the foot and the ground just after the ball bounces off the ground.

ILLUSTRATION 17   INSIDE-OF-THE-FOOT, LEG OR THIGH
TRAP—BALL COMING IN ON FLY

*Getting the inside of the foot or leg or thigh on the ball and slowing it down to
a stop is the number one job. The ball is coming in from the side at an angle.
Eye on ball—body well balanced.*

Weight on grounded foot on side ball is coming.

*Knee of trapping foot slightly bent as in stepping up—foot and leg held loosely—
trapping foot off ground.*

*Inside of trapping foot is held facing oncoming ball ready to meet it in front of
other knee.*

*On impact the trapping foot and leg are drawn back starting with outward rota-
tion from the hip to cushion the rebound.*

*A slight backward and upward rotation of the lower leg at the knee following
the preceding movement will turn the inside of the foot facing the ground and
deflect the ball into the ground.*

off the wall almost as fast as it comes in. That stone wall could be
a player's head, body or foot; hence it is imperative that all players learn how to soften, ride*, or slow up the rebound of a ball so
that it will not bounce far and out of control. To do this a player
must learn to cushion the ball and place it directly to the ground
at his feet. In cushioning the ball a player should draw back

ILLUSTRATIONS 18 AND 19   OUTSIDE-OF-THE-FOOT TRAP

A difficult trap requiring experience and confidence, but a very useful one since it can develop into a very fine combination trap and first move in any direction desired. The ball can be taken from any angle and deflected under control in any direction if the position of the foot and the distribution of the weight of the body are properly used. Eyes, of course, must be kept on the ball. The weight should be on grounded foot.

The pivot in desired direction should be made on grounded foot. The weight of the body should be leaning slightly in the direction the ball is going to be deflected. To stop the ball dead the foot and body are placed more over the ball with the foot higher off the ground so that the ball will be wedged between the outside of the foot and the ground.

slightly or give at the part of the body where the ball makes contact, and then smother it wedgelike with as much of the body as he can. For example, if a ball is coming at him waist high, at the impact he should jump slightly up and back, then draw his stomach in as if hit by a hard punch, and smother the ball by leaning over it from the waist with head, shoulders and chest.

Other salient musts in trapping a ball are keeping your eye on

ILLUSTRATION 20 (LEFT)

TRAPPING WITH CHEST
ON BOUNCING BALL

Eyes on ball.

Body directly in line behind ball. The feet on ground can be parallel or one in front of the other ready to get control of the ball when it hits the ground.

Chest on impact gives and hollows; shoulders, head and chest well over ball.

Hands and arms should be out to side for balance and eliminate any chance of hand violation.

The head, chest and shoulders literally smother the ball.

To help cushion the effect of the impact the trapper should rise on toes and draw chest and stomach in the same as in taking a deep breath.

ILLUSTRATION 21 (RIGHT)   TRAPPING FLY BALL WITH CHEST

Eyes on ball.

Body leaning slightly backward from the knees and directly in front of oncoming ball.

Feet on ground one in front of the other.

Arms out to sides.

On impact body rides the ball slightly to cushion the speed of the ball and immediately comes forward so that the rebound can be controlled.

On impact the weight of the body is on the rear foot.

ILLUSTRATION 22

TRAPPING BOUNCING BALL
WITH STOMACH

Eyes on ball.

Body directly in line with oncoming ball—feet parallel. On impact stomach is drawn in with head, shoulders, and chest drawn over the ball, hands and arms out to sides. To help in cushioning, the trapper can rise on toes or leave the ground slightly on impact as though sucking in the stomach.

When ball hits ground the player should be in a good position to take control of the ball and make an offensive move.

the ball, keeping the body directly behind the oncoming ball, proper timing, knowing exactly how to trap the ball in each particular play, and sensing what to do with it after the successful trap.

Sole-of-the-Foot Trap on Rolling Ground Ball. This is a simple maneuver used to trap a ball rolling on the ground toward the player. The only difficulty a player might encounter is when the ground is rough, causing the ball to take a crazy bounce just as the player reaches out to trap it. However, if the player positions himself correctly, that is, directly in front of the oncoming ball, he will still have a chance of stopping its forward progress with his body or legs if it does bounce.

Sole-of-the-Foot Trap on Bouncing Ball. With a bouncing ball in front of the trapper, the trap is made immediately after the ball hits the ground and is bouncing up. If it bounces a yard or so in front of the trapper and has to be played about knee high, the trapping foot is raised to deflect the ball to the ground by letting it hit the sole of the foot of the extended leg. In preference to this, drive in and play the ball with the body.

Chest Trapping. Try to get the body directly in front of the ball. The arms should be out to the sides. When the player makes contact with the ball, he rises on his toes and draws in his chest, arching the chest and shoulders over the ball. He follows through by jumping upwards and backwards to cushion the rebound of the ball. As the ball drops to the ground the player immediately moves to get control of it with his feet and to start his offensive move.

TACKLING

Most players and coaches do not consider a tackle successful unless the tackler gains possession of the ball. A tackle, in a broader sense, should not be considered a complete washout if the tackler is successful in forcing the dribbler to make a wild pass, kick the ball out of bounds or slow his forward progress so that the defense has time to cover back and reorganize itself. As in everything else, the tackler will do well if he knows his capabilities and how to use them to his advantage in the immediate situation. The tackler's moves must be intelligently based on careful study and practice.

During a game, the player must study each opposing dribbler's habits so that, when he does make his move, the chances of getting the ball will be all in his favor. Further, when the tackler does commit himself, he must know that his move is being backed up by a teammate. Although the tackler should not give ground to the extent that he finds himself backing into the mouth of the

ILLUSTRATION 23   HEAD-ON TACKLE

Eye on ball—body well over ball.

Front foot should be placed in front of the ball so that the inside of the foot is against the ball.

Weight is on front foot.

Heels fairly close together—knees slightly bent outward and loose.

If tackling with the right foot the tackler's right shoulder should be facing and opposite the right shoulder of the dribbler with the weight of the body slightly forward so that a fair shoulder block or charge can be made. The charge should be made merely to throw the dribbler off balance, not to knock him over.

Arms should be at sides to avoid being called for pushing. The ball should be blocked and held a fraction of a second and then slid by (or over) the dribbler's foot with the tackling foot (which is the front foot). This will also give the tackler the advantage by positioning his body between the ball and the dribbler.

goal, he must realize that there are situations when good judgment calls for holding up his actual play for the ball. Obviously, if a decision has to be made at the front of the penalty box as to whether to tackle or give ground, the decision can only be—tackle. The fullback or any other back should never give ground

ILLUSTRATION 24   TACKLING FROM THE SIDE

Eye on the ball—body well over ball.

If tackle is made with the right foot the left shoulder can be used in making a legal shoulder charge.

The feet are in a stride position rather than close together. Weight on tackle foot, knee well over tackle foot, ball blocked with inside of tackle foot. After blocking ball momentarily the ball is pushed forward and away from the dribbler as in the head-on tackle.

around the mouth of the goal and back into the goalie. For that matter, a player should never give ground in any other part of the field unless circumstances dictate it to be the wisest thing to do. Decisions must be based on sound judgment rather than on the applause and cheers of the crowd.

This discussion is not meant to give the reader the idea that tackling and getting the ball is frowned upon. On the contrary, the farther away from the mouth of the goal the tackle is made, once the stage has been set, the better. The discussion is merely to impress upon the reader that it isn't always the wisest move to barge in like a bull in a china closet in an attempt to get possession of the ball. If the tackler is obviously outclassed or in a situation as described above, he should play with extreme caution or he may find himself and his team looking rather ridiculous. The tackler must remember that the time to actually go in for the ball is immediately after it has been played and has left the foot of the dribbler. Everything else being equal, the man with the ball has the edge in that he can make the first move, and the reaction of the defender obviously must be a split second behind that of the offensive man. The tendency for the defender is to go with the move rather than the ball, and therefore he is open to simple feints and fakes. For this reason the tackler must be very cautious in going in for the ball and must realize the importance of timing and setting the stage for the actual tackle.

Tackling begins when the tackler makes his first move toward the dribbler and not after he actually commits himself or makes his play for the ball. The tackler's setting himself up, and getting into position to make his move for the ball, is a stage as important in the tackle as going in for the ball. Timing is essential in the actual break for it. If the tackler drives in bull-like fashion, he will very often only see the back of the dribbler. On the other hand, if he approaches cautiously, well aware of the capabilities and habits of the dribbler, and makes his play for the ball, using well-timed moves, then the chances of getting the ball are good. In sizing up a dribbler, one of the first things to look for is whether or not he always goes in the same direction when he tries to break by a would-be tackler, or whether or not he is weaker in trying to get by a would-be tackler on one side or the other. When these facts are known the tackler can wisely set himself up to meet the strength and be ready and waiting.

Perfection of tackling for the halfbacks and fullbacks is a must. One of the first requisites of a good halfback and a good fullback is being able to tackle with good judgment. In tackling a dribbler, the tackler should make his moves with sound judgment based on a thorough knowledge of the dribbler's habits, the tackler's own

ILLUSTRATION 25   TACKLING FROM THE REAR

*In making this tackle the tackler must draw up even with the dribbler and
time his move so that he is making his bid just after the dribbler pushes the
ball and for the moment presents a free ball.*

*His move must be made with the foot nearest the dribbler and his foot should
be placed between the dribbler and the ball.*

*Once he gets his foot and body in between the dribbler and the ball he merely
pulls the ball to one side and carries on from there.*

*Once he gets into this position he puts the dribbler in the awkward position of
fouling him since the dribbler will be on the tackler's back.*

*Again let me stress that the tackler should know his capabilities and that of the
dribbler or he will be outwitted.*

capabilities, his team's strengths and weaknesses, and the dribbler's possible passes and moves. The tackler should also consider
the position of his teammates and the opponent's teammates at
the time of the tackle.

Sole-of-the-Foot Tackle. Merely place the sole of the extended foot
on the ball. The tackler should assume a position directly in front
of the dribbler. Timing is essential in placing the extended foot on
the ball: Toe up, heel down, wedging the ball on the ground;

weight balanced and borne on rear foot, which is bent and firmly on the ground to brace the body on impact of ball and opponent. Momentarily hold ball and move it over the opponent's foot and away as in other tackles.

Tackling from the Rear. Although this is a dangerous tackle, a speedy player can execute it successfully. It is used, obviously, in taking the ball away from a player who is dribbling ahead and away from the would-be tackler.

The Hook Tackle. This is really a desperation effort. It is made from the side with the tackler literally reaching out with his extended leg and foot in a vain attempt to hook the ball away from the dribbler. The tackler often ends up on the ground and completely out of the play even though he does make contact with the ball. It is a dangerous skill and should not be advocated as a regular or steady method of taking the ball away from an opponent. If the tackler does hit the ball and deflect it, he usually is in no position to take advantage of it anyway. Since the advantage to the tackler is so small, it should be mentioned, demonstrated and considered well covered. There are some boys who have developed this skill to their advantage but as an ordinary run-of-the-mill skill it should not be pushed.

HEADING

The strange misconception of the beginner—that he has successfully headed a ball when he merely gets his head on it before an opponent—has greatly minimized the value of this skill as a regular and important part of a team's play. Heading a ball is a skill and should be learned the same as kicking, passing or any other fundamental. A head ball can be used as a pass to a teammate, can be hit to the ground for immediate control, bounced over an onrushing opponent's head to be immediately followed up by the header to get control; or, on defense, the ball can be headed for distance and out of danger from around the mouth of the goal.

A successful head ball does not necessarily mean one that has

ILLUSTRATION 26   **HEADING A FLY BALL WITH FEET ON GROUND**

Eyes on ball.

As ball comes toward the player he sways trunk backward from knees.

Player sets himself squarely behind the oncoming ball—weight well balanced, comfortable on feet.

The trunk coming forward must be timed so that when the head hits the ball the player is getting the most out of his trunk muscles in putting the ball where he wants it.

As the trunk comes forward the neck braces and head comes forward to hit the ball at the top of the forehead. On a head ball while the feet are on the ground the player does not snap his head forward as much as when the feet are off the ground. A good deal of the power comes from the trunk muscles.

Eyes on the ball from start to finish watching flight of ball.

The trunk and head follow through.

ILLUSTRATION 27　　　　LEAVING FEET TO HEAD FLY BALL

Eyes on ball.

If possible the body is directly in line with oncoming ball.

Timing is essential in driving hard off of one foot without breaking running stride to get height and to hit the ball at the peak of the player's jump.

Arms used to keep balance—being very careful not to foul as the player makes his jump for the ball.

Head is back with eyes always on the ball ready to snap forward at the ball with strong neck muscles.

The ball is hit at the top of the forehead. At impact the head is twisted in direction the header wants the ball to go.

ILLUSTRATION 28 (LEFT)   **HEADING BALL TO FEET**

The mechanics of this type of head ball is the same as in that of heading any fly ball with the following differences: Allow the ball to drop slightly down more and in front of the face so that when the ball is hit with the forehead it will be hit down at the header's feet.

With the usual snap of the head forward and downward (concentrate on pulling in the chin) the header will find the ball on the ground at his feet. Eyes following the flight of the ball to the ground.

Another way to play a fast ball is to bring it down quickly either to the header's own feet or that of a teammate close by is by merely riding the ball with the head, that is, on impact draw the head back to cushion the rebound.

ILLUSTRATION 29 (RIGHT)   **HEADING TO SIDE**

To bring the ball downward to the side, face the oncoming ball and hit it at the top of the forehead slightly on the side of desired direction and follow through with a downward snap of the head towards the shoulder.

been hit for distance. As a general rule the only time that the header goes for distance is when he is heading the ball away from the goal-mouth area or in any other strictly defensive situation. A successful head ball is one that is placed exactly where the header aims it. Accuracy, then, in heading as in all other fundamentals should be and must be stressed.

One of the most natural and prevalent errors a beginner makes in heading a ball is to pull in his head like a turtle when making contact with the ball. This is absolutely contrary to the best heading mechanics, since strong neck muscles must be developed to snap the head at the ball; this is the very first must in good heading. The snap of the head gives control and direction to the ball.

Another beginner's error is to head low balls. This is a very bad mistake, if for no other reason than that at such a level the ball can be played much better with the body or legs.

Timing is one of the most important musts in heading. The player must time his jump so that on impact with the ball he is at the peak of the jump. It stands to reason that, when two men go up for the ball, the one who gets to it first and highest will usually get it. Players should practice running and driving into a fly ball by taking off on one foot without breaking their stride. The eye must be always on the ball, which should be hit on the top of the forehead (or hairline) with a snap of the neck. To get direction to the left or right the player merely hits the ball on the side of the forehead and twists the head on impact in the desired direction. A quick recovery after heading the ball is important, since frequently the header is out to set the ball in position for himself; if not setting up for himself, he should be very conscious of immediately positioning himself for a pass or any other play that will give his team opportunities.

To help the ball along in the same direction, face in the direction the ball is coming and then as the ball hits the front top of head, snap head upward and backward. If you merely try to get the chin up as high and as far back as you can, you will have the perfect motion. Don't let the ball land too far back on the head or all the power will be lost.

The same purpose can be accomplished by standing at right angles to the oncoming ball and using the same mechanics as you do in heading a ball to the side.

OBSTRUCTING

Obstructing is a method of slowing the forward progress of an opponent and is best done by moving slowly forward in front of him and directly in his path. As long as the player is moving away from and not backing into the opponent, he can be sure that the block or obstruction is legal. Above all do not use the arms or hands in blocking. This rule is used wisely to prevent an opponent from making a play on a ball just before it goes out of bounds, or to make it possible for a teammate to make a clean play on the ball or take possession of it.

CHARGING

Charging is a real part of the game of soccer and should be used without restraint or fear of fouling. The discouraging thing is that the word "charge" to most people implies fouling and is looked upon as something not associated with clean playing. Charging is a subtle skill, and when used properly to unbalance an opponent is perfectly legal and will oftentimes give the charger possession of the ball. If the charger regards the charge only as a preliminary in getting the ball, rather than a way of knocking down the man, it will be helpful in making a fair charge.

Some of the points to keep in mind in making a legal charge are: keep the arms and hands in close to the body; use the shoulder in making contact; keep one foot on the ground; make sure the opponent has one foot on the ground; hit high; do not hit from the rear; make your charge when the opponent has his weight on the far foot, that is, the weight on foot farthest from you; do not charge violently.

I V

Players and Their Positions

CENTER FORWARD

The center forward is the key man on attack, yet, like any other player on the team, to be effective and to do his best, he needs a good supporting cast. A center forward can never be great or make his team great if he tries to play the game alone. A center forward must learn to fit his abilities into the team picture so that both he and his teammates will get the most opportunities for shots at the goal.

Regardless of everything, scoring of goals is the object of the game—nothing will take its place. No matter how attractive or crowd-pleasing the combination or individual brilliance is, it means nothing if a team comes out on the short end of the score.

The thrust up near the goal must be driving, varied, and frequent enough to end up with the all-important goals. An attack around the mouth of the goal that is exclusively individual is as futile as any other attack that lacks variety and imagination. A center forward can be the key in all this, but to do so his type of play must be flexible, original, impartial and versatile. He must

51

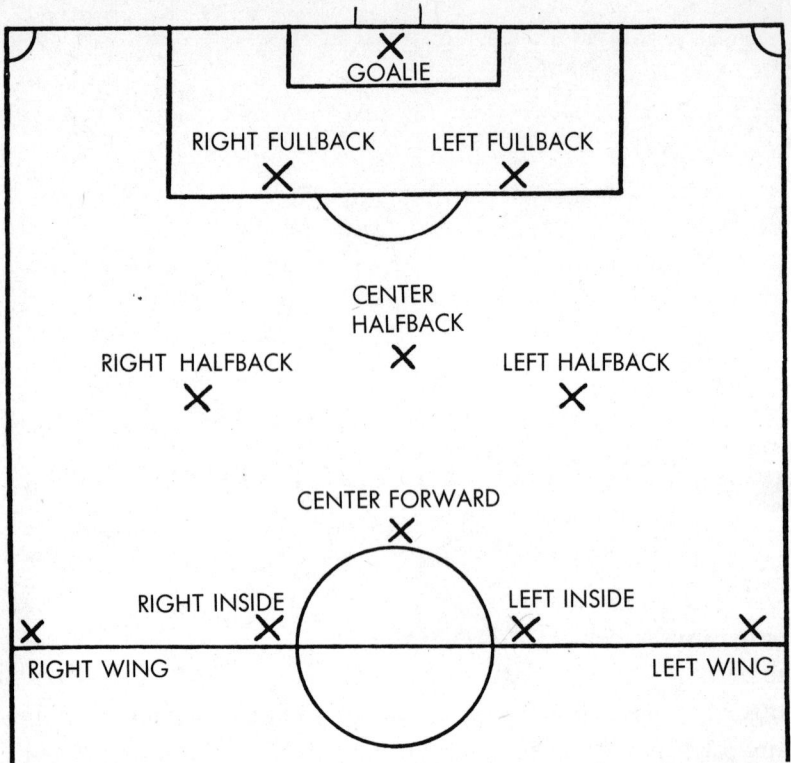

X
GOALIE

RIGHT FULLBACK   LEFT FULLBACK
X   X

CENTER
HALFBACK
RIGHT HALFBACK   X   LEFT HALFBACK
X   X

CENTER FORWARD
X

RIGHT INSIDE   LEFT INSIDE
X   X   X   X
RIGHT WING   LEFT WING

DIAGRAM 2   PLACE PLAYERS

(See opposite page 1 for key to all Diagrams.)

know the game, he must know his teammates' capabilities, and he must be constantly studying and analyzing the opponents' weaknesses and strengths to set up the easy scoring chances. He is the quarterback of the offense once the ball gets into the middle and in the opponent's end of the field. He must see openings and opportunities and play them instinctively. The players on the forward line depend a great deal on his skill and judgment. He must be constantly alert and concentrating on the game. He cannot be a prima donna and stand in one spot and expect to be effective or useful to his team. He must be constantly setting himself up for passes. The passes to him must be accurate because he is usually the closest marked man on the field.

In his play he must develop and master as many tricks as possible so that no defender will be able to anticipate his moves. By having a varied assortment of moves he will keep the defense jittery and orthodox. He must learn to go either to the right or the left and must be a deadly passer. He must make every move count and develop the ability to take advantage of any commitment by the defense. Since he is guarded very closely, he must be willing to sacrifice himself by decoying his man out of the center to open the middle for one of his teammates. Check Diagrams 25 and 28. He must be able to feint and dodge and shoot and pass off without trapping the ball, since a fraction of a second might be all the difference between getting the shot or pass-off and having it blocked.

A center forward is not the man to whom everybody passes with the idea that he has to score when he gets the ball because it is either him or nobody. On the contrary, a center forward is passed to because he is the man who can be depended on to take advantage of his own opportunities and to make and develop opportunities for his teammates. A center forward who can develop the sense or instinct of knowing when to keep the ball and when to pass off will be a great center forward, assuming of course that he has learned the fundamentals and is capable of executing them. In short, a center forward must have the cunning and ability to outsmart a defense individually and in combination to give his team the easiest and most scoring opportunities.

Positioning

On offense or defense, when the center forward doesn't have the ball, he positions himself so that, if the ball is passed to an open spot around him, he can get it and move it down to the mouth of the goal alone or in combination as quickly, directly and accurately as possible. He can make the open spots possible by jockeying his man out of position. He must follow the general rule for all players in bringing the ball up the field: get the ball into play around the mouth of the goal before the defense has a chance to organize itself. Only in special situations does he ever go farther down in the defensive end of the field than just beyond the center. His play is 99 per cent offensive.

Penalty Kicks*—Check Diagram 41.

On offense, if he is not kicking, he should try to position himself in the corner of the arc and the front line of the penalty box with his man to the outside of him. In this position he can drive in ahead of the defense for rebounds off the goalie or goalposts.

Defense is a situation in which he plays at the defensive end of the field ready to pick up clearing kicks. He must use his own judgment as to how far into the defensive end of the field he goes, keeping in mind what is expected of him. If he gets the ball on a clearing kick, he should immediately decide whether to solo or kick to a spot ahead of one of the wing forwards behind the defense. The best play is the kick ahead to a spot behind the defense for the wing forward to drive in and pick up. This quick break will open up many possibilities before the defense can get back to set up.

On a rebound the kicker cannot play the ball a second time until another man, other than the goalie, has touched it. Check Diagrams 36 through 38.

Corner Kicks*—Check Diagram 42.

On offense, he sets up in a position about six to eight yards out in front of the mouth of the goal, favoring somewhat the side of the goal away from the kicker. This will give him a chance to drive into the ball. Heading is a must in this situation and he must learn to head a ball to perfection down to either corner of the goal. His man will be playing him in a position so that he can see both man and ball and in between him and the goal.

On defense, the same as when opponent takes penalty kick.

Goal Kicks*—Check Diagrams 43, 44.

On offense, that is when his own team takes the goal kick, he should position himself around the center of the field ready to pick up any long kicks or headed passes by his insides. In positioning himself he must try to jockey his man out of the spot where he knows his teammate is trying to kick the ball. A simple set of signals should be used in all free kick situations. The offensive team should get the jump by knowing where the ball is going to be kicked. In positioning themselves, the players on the kicking team should keep in mind that it is better to drive down the field with the ball than to have to go up the field to meet it to make a play. Positioning is very important since an advantage is gained by the direction the players have to go to play the ball.

On defense, that is when an opponent is taking the kick, the center should position himself directly in front of and in line with the ball near the front line of the penalty box. He should take into consideration the kicker's ability, as well as wind, field and weather conditions, and set up accordingly. His big job is to get any goal-kicked ball he can and move in fast for a shot or pass-off. If his attempt to drive in solo is blocked, he should turn and pass off to one of the insides driving in for a shot. If the goal kick is out of his reach, he should immediately set himself up for a pass.

*Direct Free Kicks**—Diagrams 45 through 50.

On offense, the center forward should position himself so that he can get to a spot where the ball is going to be kicked ahead of the defense. If he can set himself up so that the man playing him must take his eye off of him or the ball, it will be to his advantage. If, by signal, the center forward knows that the ball is to be kicked over the heads of the defense, he should play as near to his man as he can, just on-side,* so that when the ball is kicked he can get to it ahead of his man. On free kicks near the opponent's goal, a push pass on the ground between the defensive men is very effective. So is a lob pass over the heads of the defense to either wing driving in for a play on the ball with head. The way the defense lines up will have much to do with determining the center forward's initial move in this situation.

On defense, when the kick is taken in the opponent's end of the field and midway between touch lines, he usually positions himself about ten yards directly in front of the kicker, if for no other reason than psychological. If he intercepts a poor kick he immediately makes the move that will give his team the greatest advantage. In all other situations he positions himself to get the jump on the defense and get a pass from a teammate who has intercepted the kick.

Indirect Free Kicks*—Check Diagrams 51, 52.

Play the same as direct free kicks. The following indirect free kick situations are played differently than the direct free kick situations: Check Diagrams 53 through 55.

Touch Line Kicks*—Check Diagram 56.

On offense, he positions himself near the middle of the field, the exact position depending on where on the touch line the kick is being taken. The basic principles in positioning are the same as in the free kick. He should be ready for a cross to the opposite wing inside the penalty area out of the goalie's reach or a kick down the middle, clearing the defense out of the goalie's reach.

On defense, when the kick is being taken in the offensive end of the field, he should position himself to intercept any attempted passes or kicks in his area. When the kick is taken on the defensive end of the field, he should position himself the same as he would in a corner-kick-by-the-opponent situation, ready to get the jump and to pick up any clearing kicks.

INSIDE FORWARDS

The inside forwards are the link between the halfbacks and the center forward and wing forwards. From their position on the field they can pass forward and feed either wing or center forward. An inside forward must learn not to hang on to the ball too long, since doing so gives the defense a chance to get back to cover, and makes scoring opportunities fewer and more difficult for his teammates. On the other hand, an inside forward should learn to use the dribble intelligently in drawing to set up and feed the wing forwards and center forward.

With the center forward, the inside forwards should work out simple decoy plays to open up the center. To be effective, the inside forwards should develop the knack of using variety in their attack, and work out simple combinations especially with the halfbacks, wing forwards and center forward. With variety in their offensive patterns they will make many scoring opportunities for themselves and for their teammates.

They must, like all their teammates, be sizing up the opposition so as to take advantage of their weaknesses and pack against their strengths. An inside can add a good deal to his and his team's offensive effectiveness by analyzing the halfback playing him as quickly and intelligently as possible. For example, does the half play back on defense, or does he boldly go up the field and take his shots or cross or draw and pass off? Does he make the most of his opportunities once he does get the ball in the offensive end of the field? Does he hang on to the ball and give the defense a lot of time to get back and cover? In asking these questions and in observing to get the answers, the inside forwards are adding to their team's offensive strength.

The inside forwards' strength in play should lean toward the offense, and they should be constantly trying to set themselves up to give their team the offensive edge.

Although an inside forward is very much a part of the offense, he also has a defensive responsibility. How much time and attention he devotes to each depends upon his ability to size up the opponents, and his own alertness and ability to take advantage of the opponents' weaknesses in positioning himself. The inside forwards must develop the sense of being at the right place at the right time almost intuitively. This sense is more than a matter of luck or chance, but a concentrated, intelligent study of the opponents which results in excellent positioning and control of the field and the ball.

Although the insides do have a definite position to assume on the field, they roam out of position judiciously more than the other members of the team. Because of their responsibility of being back to help on defense and because they must get up the field in good offensive position, one of the prime requisites of an inside is physi-

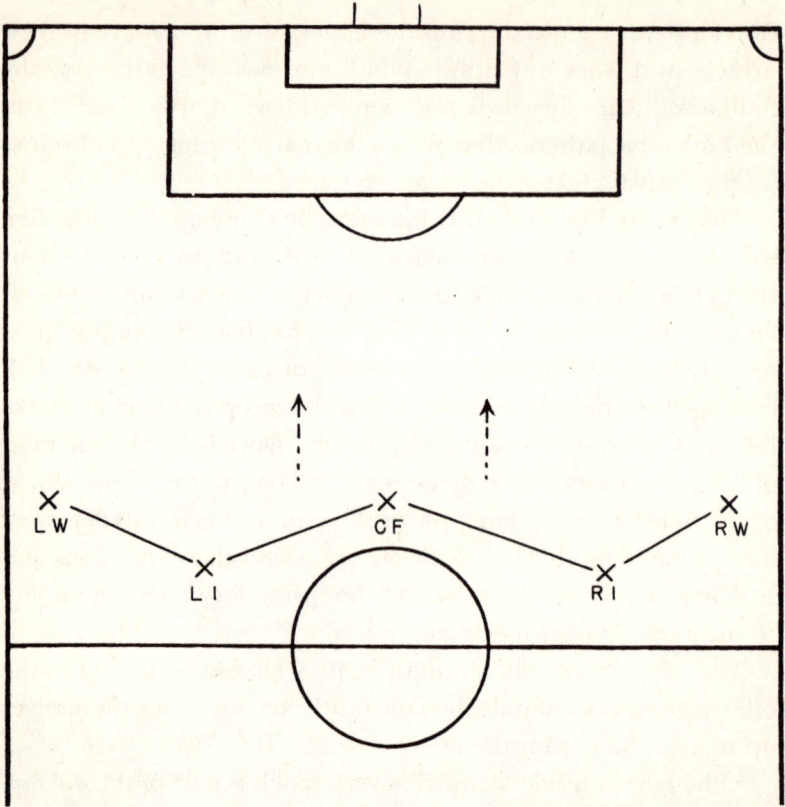

DIAGRAM 3   SHALLOW W FORMATION

cal stamina. An inside forward's leaning should definitely be offensive, and he should never make the mistake of playing the wing halfback rather than making the wing halfback play him.

If we consider the center forward and the wing forwards the first line of offense, then we should consider the inside forwards the second line of offense, but second only because of their relative positions to the center forward and the wing forwards on the field. The five forwards' basic relative positions to each other on the field form the letter "W" as in Diagram 10.

Penalty Kicks—Check Diagram 41.

On offense, if the inside forward is not taking the kick, he should position himself in the corner of the arc on the front line of the penalty box with his man to the outside of him. This will give him a good position to drive in on rebounds off the crossbar, goalposts and the goalie. At the kick he should be driving in and have it understood with his teammates who are driving in, to cover a certain area or zone. This should be flexible but the offensive men should be driving in as a wave covering all the ground and not bunching.

On defense, the inside forwards cover the halfbacks, ready to pick up any clearing kicks and making sure that the halfbacks do not get the ball and drop it back in or cross it or shoot. The inside forwards should make every effort to get the ball themselves so that they can pass it to a wing forward or to the center forward on a quick offensive thrust.

Corner Kicks—Check Diagram 42.

On offense, when the ball is being kicked from the opposite corner, he should position himself opposite the far goalpost about eight to ten yards out from the goal. He should be ready to drive into the ball and head it down into either corner. If he is the inside forward playing on the same side of the field as the kick, he should play about eight to ten yards out in front of the goalpost.

On defense, the inside forward plays the wing halfback if he is on the side where the kick is being taken, and the center halfback if he is on the side away from the kicker. His position is flexible, but he must make sure, along with the other inside forward, that the three halfbacks are covered. If the ball is kicked where he can pick it up, he should immediately kick it diagonally down the field to the corner on the same side (a cross here is a dangerous kick) where the wing forward can pick the ball up and cross or drive in for a quick scoring chance.

Goal Kicks—Check Diagrams 43, 44.

On goal kicks and free kicks the players should so position themselves in relation to each other that they are covering the maximum amount of ground without any overlapping. Accurate heading is a must in playing a goal kick.

It is wise for all players to position themselves so that on offense when they make a play on the ball, they are driving in the same direction as the flight of the ball, and on defense they are driving into the ball.

On offense, the insides position themselves around the center of the field in a shallow W formation with the wing forwards and the center forward. Their job is to get any ball between the wing forwards and center forward and aid the ball's forward progress down the field to either the wing or center forward behind the defense. The inside forwards should be thinking in terms of a fast break and in getting the ball down the field before the defense gets set up. The long accurate lead-spot pass to the wing forwards or center forward will do just that.

On defense, the inside forwards position themselves about ten yards in front of their halfbacks and set up to intercept any ball in that area. If they make a play on the ball they should be driving forward into it, covering as much ground as possible. If the inside forward makes a play on the ball, he should either drive it diagonally over the defense for his wing forward to pick up, or down the middle over the defense and out of the reach of the goalie for the center forward to pick up.

Direct Free Kicks—Check Diagrams 45 through 50.

On a direct free kick when every player has a chance to set himself up perfectly, if ever a play should be executed, it should be in this situation.

On offense, on direct free kicks in the opponent's end of the field, there are many plays that can be set up besides the usual crossing to the wing forwards or dropping the ball in the center just over the heads of the defense. These setups should be studied and worked on in practice. The inside forwards should play on a parallel line with the center forward and wing forwards just onside. In the situation with the ball being dropped over the heads of the defense, just out of the goalie's reach, the offensive team must realize and take advantage of the fact that the only opposing player driving into the ball is the goalie. With all the men driving in on him, a terrific amount of pressure is on the goalie and with it a rebound setup is quite possible. The kick over the line of defense should be out of the reach of the goalie. Also, there is just that possibility that the ball might be deflected by the goalie's driving out and into the net. In the opponent's end of the field, as a general rule, the inside forwards should play just on-side, and if the defensive line is back too far, be ready to go out for a pass in front of the line, and if the line of defense plays too far out from the goal, be ready for a lob pass over it.

When the free kick is being taken in their own end of the field (defensive end), the inside forwards play in a shallow W formation as far down the field (near the opponent's goal) as feasible, between the center forward and the wing forward. The inside forwards should try to jockey their men out of position so that when and if the kick is made to a spot in their area they will have the edge over the opponent in getting to the ball and getting control of it.

On defense, the insides should set themselves up ahead of the ball so that they can pick up any low kicks and be ready for an immediate offensive thrust. They should also be ready to pick up their assigned men on defense; the deeper the kick is in their own end of the field, the closer they play their assigned men. They should also think in terms of positioning themselves for interceptions at the logical place for the player taking the free kick to kick the ball.

Indirect Free Kick—Check Diagrams 51, 52.

Play the same as free kicks.

The following indirect free kick situations are played differently than the direct free kick situations: Check Diagrams 53 through 55.

Touch Line Kicks—Check Diagram 56.

Use the same setup on both offense and defense as in the direct free kick and corner kicks.

WING FORWARDS

Competition always drives men to get the edge which gives spice and dash to any game, but most of all it leads to changes. With competition as the driving force, we find the type of wing forward play over the years has changed from almost a one-pattern maneuver to a very interesting and flexible type of play with the use of as many patterns as the imagination can dream up and the individual's ability can master. Where a few years ago all the wing forward was expected to do was to advance the ball down the side of the field and center and cross it, now much more is expected of him. He is still expected to bring the ball down the field and center and cross it with great skill and accuracy, but, in addition, he is now expected to shoot and work in combination with other members of the team in bringing the ball down the field, and in setting other forwards up for scoring opportunities.

He must be able to dribble, pass, feint, have a good shot and know the game thoroughly. He must know when to use the cross; when to use the push pass; when and how to decoy, to clear or open a teammate for a pass and have a shot at the goal. His centers and crosses must be accurate and high enough so that there is no chance for an interception. He must learn not to solo the ball down too deep in the corner so that he finds himself fighting off an opposing halfback or fullback, and he ought to find out early in the game that the quickest way down is not always in using the dribble. He must be fast so that he can start, stop, pivot and change direction with great speed. Occasionally he must be expected to beat the defense alone.

A wing forward who does the same thing all the time will find that he will be less effective and stopped more often, before he can do the opponents any damage, than the wing who keeps the defense guessing and jittery by using more than one pattern in bringing the ball down the field. In centering, the wing forward should use his own common sense and judgment; if, for example, his forwards are small and opposing backs are big, it would hardly be advisable to send in a high center.

In setting himself up on the field he should play about five or six yards in from the touch line to give himself room to work, since the defensive man will usually play on the inside of him. Obviously, the closer he plays to the touch line the less room he gives himself to out-maneuver his man. A few years ago a wing forward hugged the touch line and never left his position; today, however, in his attempt to decoy or shake himself free of his man, the wing forward finds it wise to switch positions occasionally with the inside or center forward or even the halfback. A good wing forward will be aware of these movements and use them to his advantage. The wing forward should know and practice his fundamentals religiously and must realize that to be able to kick with either foot will add to his effectiveness.

Penalty Kicks—Check Diagram 41.

On offense, the wing forwards should play on the side of the penalty box and drive in for rebounds off the goalie, goalpost or crossbar. In driving in, the wings should make sure that they are covering a certain area. They should be cautious of the defense obstructing. They should try to jockey for a position inside of the defensive man to get the edge when driving in to play the rebounds.

On defense, the wing forward should play down the field in position ready to pick up an accurate throw from the goalie if he stops the kick and gets control of the ball or to be ready to pick up any clearing kicks. In any case, be sure to make the initial thrust a fast accurate one down the field to a spot or man behind the defense if possible. Check Diagrams 39, 40.

Corner Kicks—Check Diagram 42.

On offense, the wing forward usually takes the corner kick on his side, hence he should develop a kick that is accurate so that he will be able to drop the ball about eight yards in front of the mouth of the goal. When the kick is from the opposite side he drives in on any kick beyond the goalpost near him. Before he drives he should make sure where the ball is going so that it does not go over his head.

On defense, the wing forward plays up the field in a position to pick up any clearing kicks and start the initial offensive drive. He must know what to do and do the right thing to give his team the greatest advantage and most opportunities at the time. The initial drive must be fast and can be a spot-lead pass over the defense for the center forward to pick up or a cross over to the other wing forward beyond the defense. Check Diagrams 39 and 40.

Goal Kick—Check Diagrams 43 and 44.

On offense (when their own team is kicking the ball), the wing forwards should play around the center of the field, well positioned to pick up any kick in their areas and either set up the initial offensive thrust or be ready for a spot-lead pass down the field beyond the opponent's defense. The wing on the side opposite to where the ball is kicked should make a break for the goal (staying on-side), positioning himself to receive a cross-lead pass down the field behind the defense.

On defense (when opponents are taking kick), play depends upon the strength of the opposing team, the score, and weather conditions, such as wind and rain. If there is a strong wind against the kicker, obviously he doesn't have to get down the field to help on defense. On the other hand, if the wind is with the kicker, he should get down to help on defense. Also, if the opposing wing and inside are giving his wing halfback a hard time, he should get down and give him a hand. His helping out on defense gives the fullbacks a chance to lay back and keep the middle of the field covered and set up to stop for crosses or, in short, stop any fast breaking efforts on the part of the opponents.

Direct Free Kicks—Check Diagrams 45 through 50.

On offense, the wing forward plays in a position to receive a pass to a spot on his side of the field beyond defense. The ball in this is usually played on the head, aimed for the goal, while driving in. If the free kick is not to the wing, he immediately sets himself up for a cross or any other pass that will set him or any teammate up for a scoring opportunity.

In all these situations in the opponent's end of the field, the wing forward sets himself just on-side.

If the free kick is deep in the opponent's end of the field around the penalty box, be ready for a cross lobbed just over the heads of the defense out of the reach of the goalie, or a pass pushed in between the defense on the ground. When the kick is taken in the wings' own end of the field, he plays as far down the field as reasonable so that if a spot pass can be dropped over the heads of the defense, he will be there driving in to pick it up, or if the kick is made to land before the defense he will be well positioned to get control of the ball.

He must remember that he cannot stand still and expect to get the ball. He can either drive down, taking his defensive man with him, and buttonhook back for a pass, or wait up the field until the kick is about ready to be taken and then drive down toward the goal for a spot kick over the heads of the defense.

On defense, the wing forward should set himself in a position so that he can make a quick offensive move if the ball is intercepted and cleared by one of his teammates.

Indirect Free Kicks—Check Diagrams 51, 52.

Play the same as free kicks.

The following indirect free kick situations are played differently than the direct free kick situations: Check Diagrams 53 through 55.

Touch Line Kicks—Check Diagram 56.

Played as any free kick, however, the deeper the kick is taken in the opponent's end of the field, the more the wing positions himself as in a corner kick. As a matter of fact, some coaches prefer the wing forward to take the kick when the ball is near the opponent's goal line.

HALFBACKS

The halfbacks are considered the work horses of the team because they are as much a part of the defense as they are of the offense. They can be the cause of the defense falling apart, and they can be the reason for the success of the offense. They usually make the initial thrust on the offense, and they usually make the initial move on the defense. They can turn what looks like a quick offensive break by the opponents into a sudden and excellent scoring opportunity for their own team.

In positioning themselves, as a general rule, the wing halfbacks pivot around the center halfback. Check Diagram 16. When the ball is deep in the opponent's territory, the halfback on the strong side (side of field with ball) plays up the field in a position to work on offense in combination with the wing forward and inside. The wing halfback on the weak side (opposite side of field with ball) of the field positions himself down the field where he can intercept crosses and be ready to back the defense. On all clearings the halfbacks are expected to intercept and keep the pressure on the opponent's defense by accurately passing to the forwards or driving in for clean shots at the goal themselves.

As a general rule, the halfbacks ought to set up as in Diagram 16, since that has proved the soundest way to start a game, but their positions must be flexible enough so that a heads-up halfback can adjust his position and take advantage of the opponents' weaknesses and pack against their strength. The exact position or liberties that the halfbacks assume must be a result of correct analysis of the opponent and good judgment. A halfback must remember that he can take a good deal of pressure off the fullbacks by stopping the attack before it gets started. Halfbacks should tackle and stop the opponents before they get deep into their end of the field. Stopping a forward and taking the ball away from him is one thing, but knowing what to do with the ball, and doing it, to change the team's position from one of defense to attack, is the difference between an ordinary halfback and a good one. This first jump by the halfbacks to change the attitude of defense to offense can be done by a well-directed pass to the best placed open forward or open spot in front. Dribbling should be avoided if there is a man or spot open in front. There should be a beautiful blend of combination play between the halfbacks and forwards to set up scoring and to create a constant pressure on the opponent's defense. Halfbacks that support the forwards when they are putting the pressure on, and press the attack, make the difference between a team that scores consistently and one that scores only occasionally.

After tackling a man and getting the ball, the halfbacks must have the situation sized up so well that he gives the ball to the man who, at that particular moment, is in the best position to receive it and to get it up the field for that all-important chance at the goal.

The wing halfback can be annoying and tantalizing to the opposing wing forward by setting himself up to intercept any pass to the wing. An alert and cunning competitor can make the opponents play his game. When a halfback or any other player consistently outwits the opponent, the opponents' whole game will be thrown off. They will pass hurriedly and inaccurately and will dribble in desperation.

If the wing halfback misses a tackle on the opposing wing forward, the fullback must be ready to come out to meet the forward, with the halfback then dropping behind the fullback and positioning himself to back him or pick up his man. Check Diagram 13. If the wing halfback decides that a tackle does not seem wise at the time, he should drive his man, with the ball, out to the touch line and deep in the corner. To drive a man out to the touch line, the halfback should play ahead of the man and off, or inside of, his inside shoulder. The halfback should play ahead of the dribbler just far enough so that the dribbler will not be able to push the ball by him, or between him and the touch line, and speed down the line to pick the ball up again ahead of him. He should, of course, remember that his first object is to try to stop the speedy onrush of the wing forward, and hence tackle to nip the attack before it gets started, if possible.

The halfbacks should be determined never to be fooled twice by the same man. In playing a man, the halfbacks should approach cautiously until they learn, through carefully studying the opponent's move, the best way to tackle and to stop him before he gets deep in offensive territory. The halfbacks must be good tacklers and must be aware of all the tricks that the forward can spring on them. They must be able to size up the intentions of an opposing forward and to act with good judgment. They should never let up in trying to outwit and to anticipate their opponent. They must know when to help out a hard-pressed teammate without leaving their own men too dangerously open. The wing halfbacks are called upon for great speed because they are opposed to the speedy wing forwards on attack.

On defense they should have a definite understanding with the fullbacks on their side of the field on covering the wing forward and inside men. If the wing halfbacks have the defensive assignment of covering the wing forwards, then, obviously, the fullbacks must take the insides. In certain situations, however, a switch on covering these men is wise, and there should be an understanding beforehand as to when the switches should be made. The same understanding between the center halfback and the fullbacks should be had when the roaming type of center halfback game is played. Switches on defense allow for greater flexibility and liberties in play and with them stronger all-around team play.

The wing halfbacks are expected to intercept any crosses deep in their own end of the field by the opponents to a wing forward driving in. Check Diagram 17. They should position themselves to make sure that opposing wing forwards do not have a chance to pick up a cross behind them, and that if any cross is made they will be in a good position to intercept and clear.

Besides being able to tackle, head, trap, dribble and pass well, the halfbacks must be good shooters. Very often they get the chance—and they should make chances—to drive in and take a shot.

A halfback must be in excellent condition, since his effort is more sustained, and he works harder than any other man on the field. The halfbacks have to follow the ball more than any other player on the team. The center halfback usually does a little more roaming than the wing halfbacks. The center halfback must be an accurate feeder, a master of strategy and have a thorough knowledge of the game. He must have the knack of being dependable and always in the right spot when and where the play is the hardest. He gives the team confidence by his driving, intelligent and dependable play. He brings out the best in players by always making the play that is going to give his teammates the greatest number of opportunities. He must be able to size up a situation almost as if by intuition. His anticipation is the result of intelligent study of the opponents. Nothing is left to chance.

If the center halfback plays the third-man-back game, then his big responsibility is purely defense in checking the opponent's center forward.

Penalty Kicks—Check Diagram 41.

On offense (when own team is kicking), the halfbacks should play at a reasonable distance from the front line of the penalty box so that they are in a position first to make a play on any short kicks or headers or balls pushed out of the penalty box by the goalie. They should be ready to get the ball and shoot, cross, or lob to the wing forwards beyond the defense, or push pass on the ground between the defense to one of their forwards driving in for the pass and a shot. They must be able to reposition themselves so that they can intercept any clearing kicks to the wing forwards or down the middle to the center forward. The clearing kick in this situation will be a desperation effort with little or no accuracy by the opponents' driving in on the ball to make the play, and hence will be kicked only a short distance down the field. In setting up, the halfbacks must take this into consideration and study and take advantage of every factor.

On defense, when the opponents are taking the penalty kick, the wing halfbacks should pick up the inside forwards and try to stay inside of them so that when the wing halfbacks drive in to meet a rebound they are between their man and the goal. They should have it understood with their teammates just where they will drive in and some idea of the area they are going to cover besides covering their men. They should be driving in and covering a zone. It is a difficult play to clear the ball while driving in toward the goal without giving a corner or touch line kick. Before driving in, they should momentarily obstruct the men they are assigned to guard to give the goalie a chance to play the rebound.

The center halfback should play on either side of the penalty box near the goal line and drive in to get first the ball and then the man, assuming, of course, that his man, the center forward, is the one doing the kicking.

Corner Kicks—Check Diagram 42.

On offense, the halfbacks should play in a position so that if the ball is kicked wide or near the front of the penalty box they can either get the ball and drive in for a shot, pass off to either wing, or push pass on the ground between the defense to the center forward or insides driving in ahead of their defensive men. A pass to the wing forwards should be a lob over the heads of the defense out of the reach of the goalie. Another possibility is a pass to one of the other halfbacks who can carry on effectively from their positions. Often on a corner an alert forward will head the ball back to one of the halfbacks for a clean shot at the goal or as a preliminary move to open up one of the other scoring opportunities.

On defense, when the opponents are taking the corner kick, the wing halfback on the side of the field where the kick is being taken should stand about a yard in from the goal line on the goal area line nearest the kicker. His job is to stop any balls he can from getting by him, since a kick this close to the mouth of the goal might set up an excellent scoring opportunity for the opponents. After the kick this halfback picks up the wing forward who did the kicking, assuming, of course, that the wing forward took the corner kick.

The center halfback should play the center forward. If possible, he should play the center forward so that the latter cannot get the jump on him in driving forward into the ball. He should not let his man drive behind him and set himself up in between him and the goal. Rule of thumb is to stay between your man and the goal and keep the ball and the man in sight at all times.

The wing halfback on the side away from the kicker should pick up the wing forward and play him so that he, the wing halfback, can intercept and clear any kicks.

Goal Kicks—Check Diagrams 43 and 44.

On offense (when your team is taking the kick), the halfbacks must check the forwards and be ready to clear accurately any ball they can and send it down the field to one of their own forwards.

On defense, when the opponents are taking the kick, the halfbacks should be thinking in terms of getting the ball and driving it back into their forwards with an accurate header or kick. They should size up the situation and know exactly what they are going to do in any one of the circumstances. They should preferably set themselves up so they will be driving into the ball in making the play. It is dangerous to have the ball kicked over their heads since the play then is all to the kicking team's advantage. In setting up for this kick, the halfbacks are the third line (Check Diagram 45) and should so position themselves in relation to their insides and fullbacks that all the ground can be covered with the minimum amount of overlapping while driving forward. Since the opposing wing forward and insides in this situation must actually be played by the wing halfbacks in the attempt to stop them from making the first play on the ball, the wing halfbacks will have to use their own judgment on where they actually play. It is not wise to have the fullbacks come up and play the insides or go out and play the wing forwards since it would leave the middle in front of their own goal wide open. Their best position is around the center line of the field, give or take a few yards on either side of the line. The actual spot depends on the side of the field from which the goal kick is being taken, weather conditions, wind, score, playing time left in game, etc.

Direct Free Kicks—Check Diagrams 45 through 50.

On offense, when a team takes a direct free kick in their offensive end of the field, one of the halfbacks should take the kick. The position of the ball on the field determines which halfback kicks it. In this, the wing halfbacks should cross the ball to the opposite wing forward behind the defense or down the middle over the defense, depending, of course, on the position of the defense. A possible short pass to an open halfback might be the best play at the time for a drive in and a shot, or a drive in and a push pass between the backs to a forward driving in behind the defense. In any event, no matter what happens, there should be an understanding so that every member of the team knows where the ball is going to be placed. This kick should be an accurate pass and the beginning of a play. The center halfback can lob it to either wing forward or to the center forward, behind the defense, or push pass on the ground between the defense to a forward driving in, or pass to one of his wing halfbacks.

On defense, when the direct free kick is taken by the opponents in their offensive end of the field, the wing halfbacks must cover the wing forwards, and the center halfback, the center forward. If the ball is being kicked from one side of the field, the wing halfback on the opposite side of the field must play in a position to intercept any crosses or any attempts to kick it to a spot behind the defense for the wing forward to pick up. He should give his man a little more room and play in toward the middle of the field almost on a parallel line with him, with the idea of encouraging the kicker to kick to a spot or to his man away from the middle of the field. If the halfback positions himself correctly, he will have the advantage if the ball is kicked for the wing forward to pick up. The wing halfback on the side the kick is being taken must play his wing forward closer but still not as close as the fullbacks play the insides. The idea is to block up the middle and discourage passes into the middle in front of the mouth of the goal. The center halfback shadows the center forward. A kick down to the wing forward on the same side will put the ball into the corner and that is a good spot to have the wing forward with the ball, since a cross from there is difficult to make. On a free kick directly in the middle near the center of the field, the wing halfbacks can play on a line parallel with the goal line and again give the wing forwards a little more room by playing them loosely and towards the middle of the field. The center halfback plays behind the center forward. The distance from the goal is just enough so that if a kick is lobbed over their heads the goalie has a chance of driving out and getting control of the ball or at least punching it out of danger. The distance the wing halfbacks play from the forwards is left up to their judgment; however, they must keep in mind that a pass might come directly to their man or the ball might be lobbed over their heads behind the defense. They should always try to anticipate the play.

Indirect Free Kicks—Check Diagrams 51 and 52.

Play the same as in the direct free kick situations.

The following indirect free kick situations are played differently than the direct free kick situations: Check Diagrams 53 through 55.

Touch Line Kick—Check Diagram 56.

Play as you would in the direct free kick situations. Deep in the corner play as you would in a corner-kick situation.

FULLBACKS

Gone are the days when a player who could not play at any other position could always fit in as a fullback. Size seemed to be the only requisite for a fullback in the early days, and that mostly psychological. Today, size helps but is certainly not the deciding factor in making a fullback out of an eager beginner. A fullback must learn to be a sure kicker with either foot and have the knack of being in the right place at the right time to intercept and back up. Speed is important, if for only a short distance, to be able to recover after being outwitted.

A fullback must be intelligent and must know his game. He must be able to concentrate on and study his opponents' weaknesses and strengths. He must know how to take advantage of their weaknesses and must know how to fade off and pad his team's defense to meet the opponent's strength. In doing this he must also know his own team's strengths and weaknesses. In studying his opponents' tactics he should be able to anticipate and position himself to meet their moves almost intuitively. For every move of a forward he must learn an effective counter move. He must be able to make a quick decision based on sound judgment, and then, without hesitating, make his move. There must be a decisive, determined method about his play.

He must be consistent and dependable to the extent that he breeds confidence in his teammates by giving them the feeling that there is nothing to worry about on defense, it is in good hands. He must be steady, cool and possess an even disposition. He must learn to make his moves cautiously and strike when the odds are in his favor.

He must learn never to make the unpardonable sin of backing up into the goalie. He must realize that he should jockey his man before he makes his tackle, and that oftentimes it is better to drive the man with the ball to the touch line than it is to tackle. However, he should not back up into the penalty box under any conditions before tackling. Before tackling, the fullback must make sure, if possible, that he is being backed up and that the opponents behind him are covered. He must learn not to commit himself and try to always keep between his opponent with the ball and the goal.

He must not become an addict to sensationalism and must realize that kicking for distance should be secondary to kicking for accuracy. His one contribution to the offense is placing the ball, once he gets it, in a spot for a forward, or possibly a halfback, to pick it up. To do this, he must know where he is going to place the ball before he gets it. He must kick it to one of the wing forwards, or to the center, or diagonally to a spot in the direction of either corner so as to give his forwards time to organize themselves and a chance to get the jump on the defense. He must be a master of the volley kick and be able to first-time kick* accurately with either foot. His clearing kicks must not be high, soaring, aimless boots, but kicks to a definite spot as an initial offensive thrust. Although his kicks are usually first-time kicks, if he has a chance to stop the ball and set it up he should take advantage of the opportunity. He must learn never to kick across the mouth of the goal except as a desperation, last-ditch move.

He must be a master at heading the ball, since there are times when he cannot kick it and heading breaks up the opponent's offensive intentions. This is especially true in intercepting, with the head, on crosses and corner kicks. He must always keep his eye on the ball in retreating and only in unusual circumstances, dribble. He should never be tackled with the ball.

The duty of the fullback is to defend. In setting up to defend, his moves and position on the field must blend in with those of the other men on the defense, especially the other fullback, the wing halfback on his side of the field, the center halfback and the goalkeeper. The fullbacks and the goalkeeper should be constantly working together as a unit; and with every aggressive move one fullback makes, the other should be moving to back it up. Although the fullbacks and goalie work as a unit, the fullbacks must also be working and have a positive understanding with the halfbacks on every possible play situation. Many goals are scored through a misunderstanding between the backs and the goalkeeper. These three should, through study and practice, have a definite understanding as to what their job is in every conceivable play situation. They should always be ready to back up each other's moves. The fullbacks must give the goalie plenty of room to see the ball and to work. They must never crowd the goalie, and must give him the play when he calls for it.

The fullbacks should play one ahead of the other, in tandem, backing each other up on all plays. Their position up the field depends upon where the ball is on the field. When the forwards are attacking, the forward fullback should be in a position so that on a clear by an opponent he can pick up and lob the ball back in to an open spot or uncovered forward. Better than defending one's own goal is preventing the opposition from getting away from their own end of the field. A fullback up the field can nip many an attack before it gets started.

In a situation where the fullback finds himself faced with the problem of stopping two onrushing forwards, he must concentrate on delaying and setting himself up to intercept a pass from one to the other. He must try to make the man with the ball commit himself, and keep aware of the fact that the ball can be lobbed over his head to a spot for the other forward to drive in and pick it up. He should try to jockey the man with the ball into hurrying a pass, or into taking a wild shot at the goal, or draw the two men together so that he has a chance to make a play on the ball, or give the goalie a chance to play the pass. The goalie in this case should anticipate the pass and make his break to the ball if the pass is made. Check Diagram 8. In playing the two men, the fullback should play nearer the forward without the ball so that if a ball is lobbed over his head he has a better than even chance of intercepting or deflecting. He should not make the unpardonable error of driving immediately out away from the middle without sizing up the situation behind him, since this will leave the middle of the field wide open for a lob-spot-lead pass over his head to the second forward and a clean open shot at the goal.

The fullbacks must keep the middle of the field covered.

Penalty Kicks—Check Diagram 41.

On offense, when the fullback's team is doing the kicking, both fullbacks play up around the middle of the field and if the kick is unsuccessful and the ball is cleared they then set up to meet and stop any fast break by the opponents. The front fullback of the tandem is on the side the ball is cleared, the other fullback drops back ready to back up, to cover the middle and to intercept any crosses.

On defense, when the opponents are taking the free kick, the fullback should play between the man he is assigned to cover and the goal. It will be either the wing forward or inside. He should not let his man set up inside of him, between him and the goal. If he does, it will give his man the edge on going in for a rebound. His first move after the kick is to obstruct the forward progress of his man so as to give the goalie a chance to play a possible rebound. He then drives in to try to clear if the goalie cannot handle it.

Corner Kicks—Check Diagram 42.

On offense, both fullbacks play up around the center of the field in a position to control all clearing kicks by the opponents and ready to place the ball back into the forwards and keep the pressure on the opponents' defense.

On defense, the fullbacks check the insides. It is important that the fullbacks, in playing their men, never lose contact with them. The fullbacks should not make the fatal mistake of being jockeyed out of position, hence giving their men the advantage of position in this situation. Rule of thumb is for the fullbacks to stay inside of their opponents, try to get position and always keep their eye on the ball and their man. Heading the ball out of danger in this situation is a must.

Goal Kicks—Check Diagrams 43 and 44.

On offense, if one fullback takes the kick, the other fullback plays almost on a parallel line with the ball to the inside, in front of the goal, ready to cover the middle, any crosses, or come out and stop any sudden offensive thrust on intercepted balls by the opposing center forward or insides. If the goalie takes the goal kick, the one fullback plays the center forward on the front line of the penalty box and the other fullback plays in the mouth of the goal, favoring the side from which the goal kick is being taken.

On defense, the fullback on the side the ball is being kicked plays near center of field, ready to stop any immediate drive by intercepting the ball and passing it back to one of his own men up front. The other fullback, who is playing on the opposite side of the field from which the ball is being kicked, plays nearer his own goal, ready to come up and stop any opponent's offensive thrusts on his side and in a position ready to cover any crosses, cover the middle and back up the other fullback.

Direct Free Kicks—Check Diagrams 45 through 50.

On offense, when the kick is taken in their own end of the field, one of the fullbacks takes the kick and the other fullback is back ready to cover the middle and crosses in the event of a poor kick and loss of ball. The fullback kicking should try to drop the ball to a spot for either wing forward to pick up or, if the middle is open, a spot-lead pass for the center forward to pick up. In taking these kicks the fullback must analyze the opponents' weaknesses and hit them. The fullbacks should take these kicks up to the center of the field and under certain conditions beyond the center, especially with the wind and in wet weather. In both situations the ball should be dropped around the mouth of the goal.

When the kick is taken in the opponent's end of the field, the fullbacks set up to nip any sudden thrust.

On defense, when the kick is taken in their end (defensive end) of the field, the fullbacks play on a line parallel to the goal line, checking their own men out far enough in front of the goal so that if a kick is lofted over their heads the goalie can make a play on it, and not back too far so that the opponents can push pass or drop the ball to an opponent in front of them to the opponent's advantage. The fullbacks should know and be ready for all possibilities on all free kick situations and be very aggressive in all.

When the kick is being taken near the front of the penalty box, the fullbacks can either play their own men as near the ball as possible or, with the halfbacks, form a defensive line about arms length from each other directly in front of the ball on a line directly to the middle of the goal. In any case they must set up so that the goalie has his eyes on the ball throughout the play. The fullbacks must be aggressive and make the first play on the ball and make sure not to back up into the goalie. If the ball is lobbed or kicked over their heads they should obstruct and slow the forward progress of their own men to give the goalie the chance of making the play on the ball. When the goalie knows that he is being supported by his fullbacks it gives him more confidence in going out unhesitatingly to make the play. On a free kick on the front line of the penalty box, the backs must be cautious of a pass pushed between them on the ground for the opposing forwards driving in to make a play on it. When the kick is being taken by the opponents in their end of the field, the fullbacks use their own judgment in setting up, always basing their judgment on the two principles of not setting up too far back so that a pass can be kicked in front of them and not too far out so that the goalie cannot make a play on the ball before an opponent if it is lobbed over the fullbacks' heads. In setting up for this, some teams play the offside rule to their advantage.

Indirect Free Kicks—Check Diagrams 51 and 52.

Play the same as a direct free kick.

The following indirect free kick situations are played differently than the direct free kick situations: Diagrams 53 through 55.

Touch Line Kicks—Check Diagram 56.

Played the same as a direct free kick. On offense and defense, the nearer the goal line the kick is taken, the more the setup is like that of a corner kick.

GOALIE

From a spectator's point of view, the goalie usually looks like the man on the field who has the least to do. He is the man on the team who, doing nothing, leans on the goalpost when the ball is at the other end of the field and who, when the ball comes down to his end of the field, occasionally has a stop to make; it must be easy, since so few shots get by him. That is exactly what a spectator should see, a relaxed, confident goalie with the ball up at the other end of the field, and a cool, calm player always in the right position playing and stopping shots with a tremendous amount of sureness and little effort.

From a player's point of view, however, what is going on in the goalie's mind when the ball is up at the other end of the field, and when the ball is coming down the field, and when it is about ready to be hit for the mouth of the goal is somewhat more involved. An effective goalie, to begin with, is a player who, through constant, intelligent study and practice, will position himself and make the play when it presents itself almost as though it were intuition. A

good goalie leaves nothing to chance. He works out every possibility and when a situation comes up the element of chance is re-
duced to a minimum.

He knows what to do when the wing crosses the ball, what to
do when a forward comes at him on a breakaway solo or a breakaway with a teammate, when to leave the goal, where best to position himself in the mouth of the goal on every conceivable play
and from every conceivable angle. He knows when to punch the
ball, when to catch it, when to throw it, when to kick it, how to
play the wind, how to play a wet ball, how to play a ball curving in, when to dive, when to feint, and when to give a corner.
These skills just don't happen to a man or boy who plays the goal;
they are, obviously, the result of natural ability combined with intelligent study of the position and the game and earnest, determined and persistent practice.

The man who looks as though he has nothing to do in the
mouth of the goal during the game is constantly studying his opponent's moves individually and as a team. He watches and
studies the players on the forward line and analyzes their weaknesses and their strengths and then plays them accordingly. He
studies their moves so that he can anticipate them and position
himself to make an easy save out of what ordinarily might be a
score. He eliminates desperation chances through study and
thereby keeps the percentages always on his side in every move he
makes. He studies the center forward's moves so that he knows exactly when the center forward passes off and to which side,
whether he can shoot with only his right foot or both, whether
he is a clever dribbler, and whether he hits the ball only after he
traps and gets control of it or hits the ball without trapping it.
Does he ever head the ball and how good is he when he does?
Is he a good team man or does he tend to solo? The goalie studies
the insides as determinedly, carefully and thoroughly as he does
the center forward. He studies the wing forwards the same way
and comes up with answers: does the wing usually cross and how,
does he wait until he gets deep or does he cross it far out, does he

try to get by the back and come in for an occasional shot? The halfbacks—what can he expect from them? Do they come in often and take shots, or do they keep feeding the forwards and let them do the shooting? How does the halfback feed the forwards—by crossing in the air or by trying to push the ball on the ground between the opposing backs to an open spot so that the forwards can drive in on the ball for a shot? Those are a few of the things a heads-up, wide-awake, very-little-scored-upon goalie is thinking about during the game.

The goalie is more or less the general of the defense. He is always helping his backs by talking to them, to set them up in the best possible defensive position. His job is unique in that there is no one in a position to back him up as there is in every other position. If a ball gets by the goalie, and it's surprising how very few do, the score is exaggerated many times because of its significance. Because of this, a goalie must be so constituted mentally that he is not easily upset, but is capable of reorganizing himself quickly, ready to do his best no matter what happens or when it happens. He should never make the same mistake twice. After a mistake he should learn that he must get back in the game with more dogged determination than ever not to let the ball get by him, and chalk his mistakes up to progress in becoming a top-notch goalie.

He should study and know his own team's individual and team weaknesses and strengths so that he can take advantage of the strengths and help cover and support the weaknesses. His word around the mouth of the goal must be law. His duties are almost 100 per cent defensive. The only time he is on the offense is when he throws or kicks the ball forward to a teammate.

In looking for a boy to develop into a real goalie, a coach must find one with some natural ability and certain physical and mental qualities. A boy must have good eyesight and hearing, the ability to make quick and sound decisions, and a willingness to work hard. He must be able to handle the ball. He must be alert, agile and cool. He must anticipate. He should be bold and daring.

ILLUSTRATION 30   WELL-BALANCED STANCE OF GOALIE
IN MOUTH OF GOAL

Finally, he should possess the quality of not letting himself become overanxious so that anxiety is his undoing.

There are certain fundamentals regarding the mechanics of the goal position that are not characteristic of any other position and must be learned through vigorous practice. The most important fundamental is handling the ball. A goalie must be able to handle the ball so that he can get control of it, keep control of it, get rid of it accurately to his team's advantage with little or no danger of losing it. He must learn how to cushion the impact of a hard shot directly at him on the ground and in the air. He must learn how to get his body behind the ball, so as to cushion the force of the shot, and he must use his body and legs as safety valves in case the ball gets through his hands.

In assuming his position in the mouth of the goal, before the ball is kicked at the goal, the goalie should learn to maintain a well-balanced position so that he will always be able to drive,

ILLUSTRATION 31   DIVING

equally as well, in any direction. In maintaining this well-balanced position when moving right, the goalie should move his right foot in that direction first and follow by pulling the left leg up so that the weight of the body is always evenly distributed on both feet. This is called the shuffle or glide movement. The advantage of the shuffle movement is that balance is always maintained and this sets the goalie ready to go in any direction.

In going for a ball where the goalie cannot get his body behind it, he should reach out with his arms and hands, with the palms of his hands facing the ball. If it is too far out for both hands, he should reach well out with the hand which is most natural for him, and follow up with the other hand, bringing the ball immediately into the body, if possible. If the ball is too far off for either hand to get control, then the goalie will have to resort to a dive which usually ends in punching the ball. The goalie should always dive at an angle away from the goal so that if the ball has to be punched it will clear the mouth of the goal and not hit the goalpost. After the dive, the goalie should make it a habit to get to his feet quickly. In punching the ball, the goalie should make sure that he does not punch it into an onrushing forward. He should punch the ball hard away from the mouth of the goal and toward the touch line.

The following section deals with the fundamentals of playing the ball as it comes to the mouth of the goal from all angles and levels.

ILLUSTRATION 32   MECHANICS OF FIELDING
OR HANDLING A GROUND BALL

Eye on ball.
Body directly behind the ball in line with the flight of the ball.
Hands cupped—arms outstretched.
Goalie down on one knee.
Foot of knee on ground well under buttocks.
Knees of both legs bent slightly outward.
When ball hits hands the hands and arms give to cushion the effect of the impact of the ball and the ball is brought into the pit of the hollowed stomach with the chest, shoulders and head well over the ball.

Once the goalie has the ball under control he should learn to get up and get rid of it as quickly and accurately as possible. The throw or kick should be diagonally forward to the side to one of his own teammates.

In going to either side on a ground ball, the goalie should try to get in position behind the ball as quickly as he can and then field it as he would any ground ball coming directly at him.

Mechanics of handling a ball coming in at the goalie head high: Eye on ball; get body directly behind ball; hands cupped, palms facing oncoming ball, arms outstretched, reaching; goalie should grasp the ball and pull it down into pit of stomach, chest

OPTIONAL WAYS FOR GOALIE
TO FIELD OR HANDLE A
GROUND BALL

and shoulders arched over ball; the goalie should quickly regain
balance and get rid of the ball. An optional way of playing a ball
coming in head high is for the goalie to time jump upward and
play the ball as he would a chest-high ball.

Throwing the ball: An accurate throw to an open teammate is
a wiser move than a long kick "with a prayer." A goalie should
practice throwing a ball just like he would a baseball in from the
outfield. The throw is a long one like the outfield throw, not a
snap throw like a catcher's to second. Things to remember in
throwing are: Get the full swing of the arm; at the start of the
throw put full weight of the body on the rear foot, rear leg
slightly bent; front foot almost directly in line and in front of rear
foot; body is leaning slightly backward; to get the full benefit of
the body and arm start forward motion with chest; follow through
with hand and foot pointing in direction the goalie wants the ball
to go, weight on front foot.

Angle of Possibility: The angle of possibility merely gives the
shooter an idea of the difficulty of his shot and the ultimate pos-

MECHANICS OF HANDLING A BALL
COMING IN AT THE GOALIE
WAIST HIGH

Eye on ball.

Body directly behind flight of ball.

Hands cupped and arms outstretched.

Body well balanced on feet.

Feet can be in either parallel or tandem line—individual preference.

When the ball hits the hands, the hands and arms give to cushion the effect of the impact of the ball and the ball is brought into the pit of the hollowed stomach with the chest, shoulders, and head well over the ball.

Once the goalie has the ball under control he should learn to get rid of it as quickly and accurately as possible, usually diagonally forward to a teammate.

sibility or chance of his scoring. The angle is arrived at by drawing two straight lines from the shooter—one to each goalpost. The angle formed by the lines meeting at the shooter is called the angle of possibility. The size of the angle indicates the degree of diffi-

ILLUSTRATION 36   MECHANICS OF HANDLING A BALL
                        COMING IN AT THE GOALIE
                                      CHEST HIGH

Eye on ball.
Get body directly behind the ball.
Hands cupped, arms outstretched.
On impact of the ball the goalie's hands and arms give, bringing the ball into
the chest. The head, shoulders and chest are arched over the drawn-in ball which
gives the goalie firm control of the ball against his chest.

culty of each shot. The larger the angle the greater the possibility
in favor of the shooter. As the angle gets smaller, the smaller or
more difficult the chances for the shooter to score. A study of
angles gives the goalie a definite factor in positioning himself in
the mouth of the goal to play the shot.

The following diagram shows the shooting angle possibilities
from spots in front of the goal. As the reader would suspect, the
largest shooting angle possibility is presented to the shooter when
taking a shot directly in the middle of, and in front of, the mouth

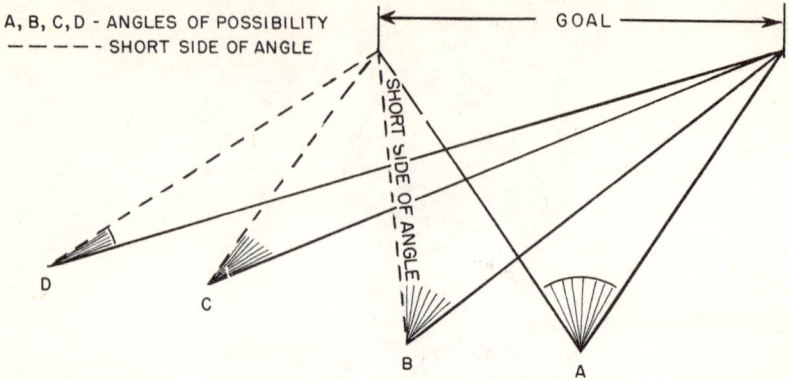

A, B, C, D - ANGLES OF POSSIBILITY
— — — — - SHORT SIDE OF ANGLE

GOAL

SHORT SIDE OF ANGLE

D

C

B

A

DIAGRAM 4   ANGLES OF POSSIBILITY

Angles of possibility of shots taken from various spots. Please note how the · angle becomes smaller as the shots are taken farther away from the spot directly in front of the middle of the goal mouth. In positioning himself for the shot the goalie should play about one yard or more in front of the goal line always favoring the short side of the angle, which is the broken line in the diagram. Although the angle of possibility does not, per se, change when a goalie drives out to meet the onrush of a forward driving in solo for a shot, it is a fact that, the nearer the goalie gets to the ball the better chance he has of stopping or deflecting it, because he has less ground to cover to each side of him to stop the ball and also when driving out he can drive to either side a greater distance.

of the goal. Any shot taken to either side of this spot presents a smaller angle and, hence, a smaller chance of the shooter scoring. The farther the shooter takes his shot from the middle, the smaller the angle and the less his chances are of scoring.

On playing a ball coming in at an angle, the goalie always makes sure that he has the goal covered on the short side of the angle. He should always stand about one yard in front of the goal. As a matter of fact, he can give a few feet on the short side and still have the percentages in his favor. Often when the shooter does try to kick or place the ball just inside of the goalpost, he goes wide of his mark. The goalie can usually tempt a shooter into this shot and make him miss. However, with a wide space open on the long side of the angle, for some psychological reason, the shooter will take the shot at this side of the goal, in spite of the fact that it is a poorer percentage shot for him.

Free-Area Angle Possibility

Another method for both the shooter and the goalie to analyze the possibilities of shots, using the angle as the gauge, is to consider the free-area angle possibility which presents the size of the open or free lanes for the shooter to drive the ball past the goalie. This is based primarily on the amount of ground the goalie cannot cover to either side of him in the mouth of the goal, and the position he assumes in relation to the position of the ball when shot. From this the shooter will learn what part of the goal is best for him to shoot at to score, without stopping to think or look. It helps the shooter develop an intuitive reaction which is a timesaver and

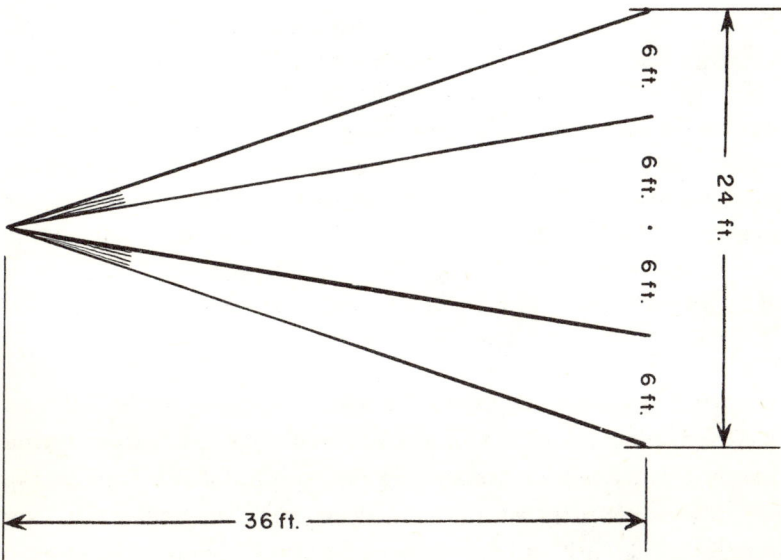

DIAGRAM 5   FREE-AREA ANGLE POSSIBILITIES
The blacked-in area gives the free-area angle possibility for a shooter to score assuming that the goalie can cover six feet on either side of him. Obviously, assuming everything else is equal, the goalie who can cover more ground to either side of him will definitely guard the goal more effectively and make more saves.

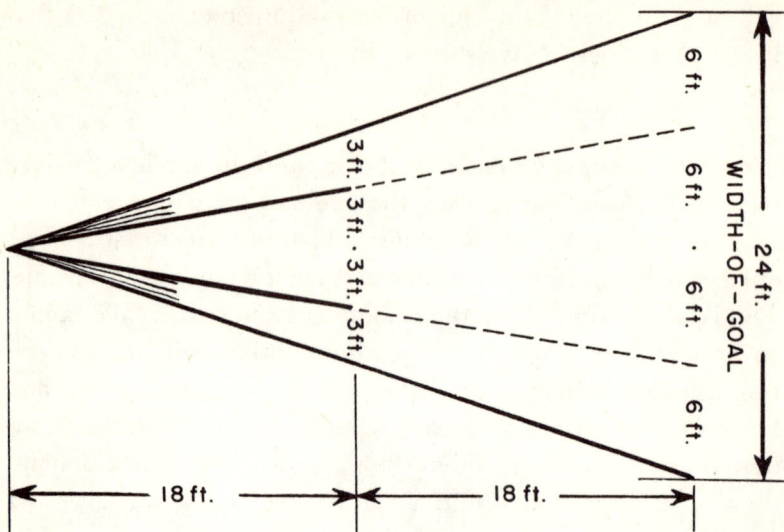

DIAGRAM 6   CUTTING DOWN ON FREE-AREA ANGLE
POSSIBILITY BY COMING OUT
TO MEET THE BALL

The blacked-in area shows the free-area angle possibility after the goalie comes out and cuts the distance between him and the shooter in half. Obviously, the angle itself does not change in this situation, but it is a fact that the closer the goalie gets to the ball the smaller becomes the goal area that he cannot cover and, hence, the chance of stopping or deflecting the shot swings in his favor. What the goalie does is literally cut the width of the goal in half and the scoring chances of the shooter down proportionately.

oftentimes the ultimate difference between getting the ball off and having it blocked. This will also prevent the shooter from giving his shot away, which constitutes deception. Check Diagram 5.

On a drive-in by an unguarded forward, the goalie must act boldly, confidently, and with as much good judgment as he can, to go out and meet the ball and make a successful play. By going out, the goalie hurries the forward into committing himself and does not give him a chance to pick the time and the spot to place the shot. He puts as much pressure on the forward as he does on himself by making the forward make a hurried decision

ILLUSTRATION 37   MECHANICS OF HANDLING A BALL
COMING IN AT THE GOALIE
OVER HIS HEAD

Eye on ball.

If possible, the body should be in direct line with flight of oncoming ball.

The palms of the hands should be facing the ball so that when the ball hits the hands if the goalie cannot get control of it he at least will stop its forward motion. The one trouble with this is that a soft rebound might be the result and a goal for a hard-driving opposing forward.

The other possibility is to tap or flick the ball over the crossbar with both hands or fists making sure that the ball is given plenty of clearance. This is in preference to giving the onrushing forwards an easy soft rebound to play.

Punching or striking the ball away from the goal and toward the touch line is another alternative.

and a hurried shot. A delayed decision by the goalie might find him still in the goal when the forward takes the shot, with percentages in the forward's favor.

The answer to when the goalie should make his move is: to get out as fast as he can to meet the player, using as much caution as the situation allows, combined with good judgment and all the confidence that he can muster. This doesn't mean to run out and meet the onrushing player for the sake of meeting him.

ILLUSTRATION 38 (LEFT)   **PUNCHING**

In punching the ball with clenched fists the force comes from extension of the arms. The ball should be hit with the knuckles; the goalie can punch the ball with one or both fists. The goalie should punch when there is no other possibility of getting his hands on it, and control, especially when he is surrounded by opposing players.

The hands start usually from in front of the chest, face, or head.

ILLUSTRATION 39 (RIGHT)   **STRIKING**

Striking differs from punching in that the ball is hit with the side of the clenched fist or fists and the motion starts with the hand or hands at the side of the head.

It means to get out there to get his hands on the ball so as to get possession of it, deflect it so that the forward will lose control and his chance at the goal, or hurry the forward into making a poor decision so that he will take a wild shot.

Usually, on a drive-in solo, the forward has just broken away from or by a back and is moving into the penalty-area box. An inexperienced player coming in will, as soon as the goalie makes his dash forward, get his shot off quickly and hurriedly; however, when the more experienced player sees the goalie coming toward him, although he might not take his shot right away, he will change his whole attitude from complete confidence of merely having to take a shot to how am I going to beat the goalie for my shot? With this, the pressure is just as much on the dribbler as on the goalie since he has to make the decision and the move with the ball.

With each step the goalie takes toward the oncoming forward, it becomes more difficult for the shooter to get the ball by him. The goalie should not give the forward a chance to organize his wits and decide on his move.

When the goalie goes out after the oncoming forward, the forward might try to shoot, dribble by or lob the ball over the goalie's head. If he takes his shot, fine, it will be a hurried one, and since the goalie is driving forward, he has gathered speed to go to either side a greater distance than if standing still. If the forward lobs coming in at full speed with the goalie rushing him, his chances of success are pretty slim since it is almost impossible to gain the height necessary to clear the goalie with outstretched hands.

If the forward tries to dribble by as soon as he gets within five or six yards of the goalie, the goalie must go after the ball. The goalie should keep his eyes on the ball and, with a catlike move, go after it with his hands and arms outstretched so that if he cannot get control of it, he will deflect it with the hope of completely spoiling the opponent's chance of taking a shot. Speed is all-important. The goalie should not make the fatal mistake of kicking at the ball.

On a breakaway by a wing forward, the same procedure should be followed although the danger isn't as great. The goalie should go out in a direct line with the oncoming wing forward and in a position favoring the short side of the angle. The goalie should al-

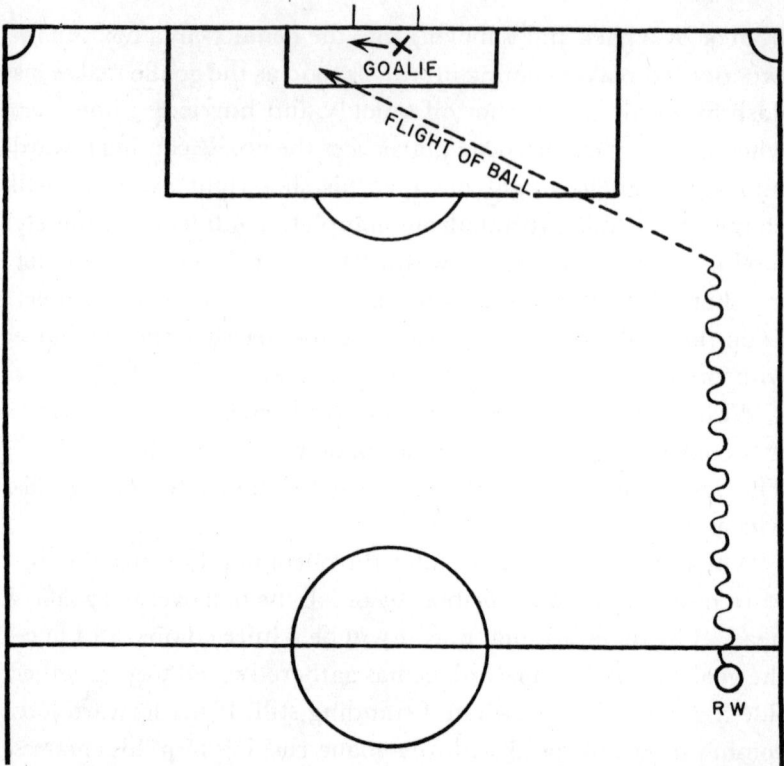

DIAGRAM 7   POSITION OF GOALIE ON CROSS

The advantage of the goalie in positioning himself about three or four feet in front of and about one yard in from the near goalpost on a drive-in shot or a cross by the wing forward seems quite obvious, in that the wing forward coming in to take this shot finds himself faced with driving the ball between the goalpost and the goalie or in the open mouth of the goal behind the goalie. In either case the goalie has the advantage. First, because he positions himself to handle the shot between him and the near goalpost and if the wing takes a hard shot at the goal mouth behind the goalie it will, according to all laws, clear the crossbar. If the wing forward decides to cross the ball, the goalie has the opportunity of getting his hands on it as it crosses, which should be the number one move, if possible. Secondly, if the ball is successfully crossed to a player driving in on the opposite side, the goalie still can retreat and get into position fast enough for a play. However, the goalie should not drive over too fast and have the ball headed right by and behind him into the nets. The goalie, then, on a cross, places himself almost in front of the goalpost about a yard in front on the side the ball is being brought down by the wing. As the ball crosses most completely obscure the side of the goal near him, and if the wing forward attempts a shot past him at the long side of the angle, the chances are very slim that he will be able to score.

When two forwards come at the goalie on a breakaway, the goalie should drive out quickly with good judgment about seven or eight yards and try to jockey the man with the ball into making a pass. If he does make a pass the goalie has a chance to intercept. He must remember that with two men bringing the ball down, the obvious thing for them to do is to draw him out of position if possible; hence, the goalie should, in driving out, be aware of this and do all he can to feint the man with the ball into making a pass and be in position to intercept it or make a play on it before the pass receiver has a chance to get the ball under control.

The following are a few do's and don'ts for the goalie to mold into his goal playing and thinking habits. They should save him many uneasy moments and make his play in the goal much more effective.

He must eliminate the soft rebound.

He should be one jump ahead of the opponent; anticipate but base it on study, practice and good judgment.

He should remember that no two opponents are alike.

The goalie is the last line of defense. He must be philosophical about being scored on and be mentally set and alert to outwit opponents and stop the next shot.

He must be confident that he can stop anything that comes his way.

---

in front of the goal he goes along with it keeping his eye on it all the way. If there is any chance of getting control of it, or punching it as it comes across the goal mouth he should by all means do so. Playing the ball as it comes across the goal, on a cross, can in many instances, be the difference between saving a goal and not saving a goal. Letting the ball go across gives the opponents a chance to make a play and a possible score. This calls for good and instant judgment on the part of the goalie and is one of the most important plays to be made by him.

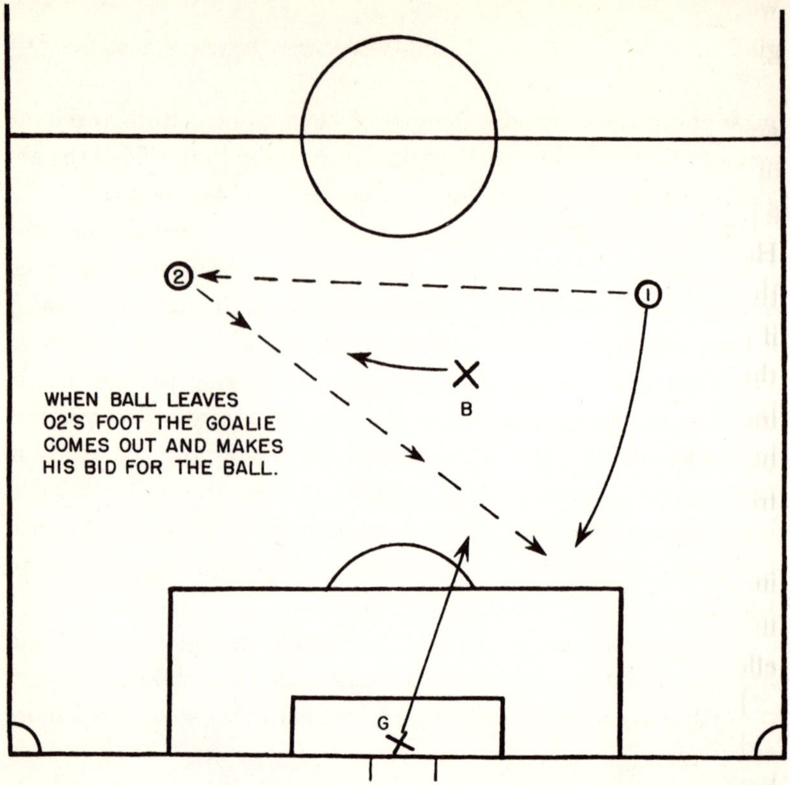

WHEN BALL LEAVES
02'S FOOT THE GOALIE
COMES OUT AND MAKES
HIS BID FOR THE BALL.

DIAGRAM 8   GOALIE ANALYZING AND BREAKING UP
                         PLAY BEFORE IT DEVELOPS

There is great strength in favor of a goalie who is constantly analyzing and diagnosing plays as they shape up and, hence, is able to stop them before they do develop. For example, in this diagram an alert goalie will see the play shaping up when O1 passes the ball to O2 and O1 starts to make a break behind XB. When O2 sends a lead pass behind and by XB to cutter O2, the goalie immediately makes his break out to the ball with the hope of either intercepting or preventing O1 from really getting control of the ball, or hurrying O1 into a wild shot or an attempted repass to O2 who should be covered by XB. Staying in goal while O1 receives pass, obviously, means trouble for the goalie.

He must make effective use of his hands.

He must be a sound workman and give confidence to his teammates.

He should display ease and confidence in handling shots.

He should never get panicky.

He should never let a high lob bounce in front of him, but should go out and get it before or just after the bounce.

He should play each shot as though the game depended on a save.

He should keep his hands warm in cold weather.

He should practice with a wet ball.

If a goalie has to dive, he should dive diagonally forward, push the ball if he cannot get his hands on it, and after the dive, get to his feet quickly.

He should never take a flying kick at the ball unless in desperation. He should use his hands and increase safety by getting his body behind the ball.

The goalie does not have to move far but should learn to move quickly when he does.

He should gather the ball first in his arms, then into body.

He should fall on the ball only as a last resort.

A goalie should practice his weaknesses.

He must be able to judge the effect of wind on the ball, the speed and spin of the ball.

He must be good judge of distance and motion.

He should punch the ball when surrounded by opponents.

He should not bounce the ball any more than he has to, especially in wet weather.

It is fatal for a goalie to make up his mind, make a move and then change his mind. He must learn to make one decision, and with study, practice and experience it should be the right one.

He should throw in preference to kicking since it is more accurate.

He should clear the ball diagonally to the side.

He should remember to always have the ball coming towards him and remember that anything in the goal area is his ball.

If the goalie goes in the air surrounded by players and there is not a chance of holding the ball, he should punch the ball.

He should catch the ball and get control of it whenever possible.

Penalty Kicks—Check Diagram 41.

On defense, the goalie plays midway between the goalposts with both feet on the goal line well balanced, ready to make a play to either side of him. Unless he is absolutely sure of what the kicker will do, he should play in the center and wait for the kick.

On the penalty kick, the goalie must look at the percentages logically and then use intelligent and sound judgment in making his moves. From a well-balanced position in the center of the goal, the goalie should be able to cover at least five or six feet to either side. Another two feet could be added to each side with a dive and either a grab or a punch. That leaves about four feet at each end of the goal open for the shooter. With the pressure on the shooter, who obviously is trying to shoot it as close to the goalpost as he can, and as hard as he can, the chances of error are very possible. Hence, unless the goalie has good reason to know the habits of the kicker, he has as good or better chance of stopping it if he plays in the middle of the goal than if he tries to outguess or anticipate where the kicked ball is going. In anticipating, the move should be not just a guess, but be based on definite observation or information, such as watching the kicker during pregame practice, seeing the player kick previously, or on information passed on by a scout or players of another team who have seen the player kick during a game with them.

Corner Kicks—Check Diagram 42.

On defense, the goalie plays facing the kicker, either on or a couple of feet in front of the goal line, with his back to the far goalpost and the open mouth of the goal and the play in front of him, the assumption being that it is easier to drive forward to play the ball than to play it while moving backward. He should move any player to make sure that he never loses sight of the ball and that his forward progress to make a play on it will not be blocked.

The goalie should watch the curve on the ball and not be fooled in coming out to play a ball that is curving away from the mouth of the goal. On the corner kick, using the punch is very ordinary since the goalie is often surrounded by opponents while jumping in the air to play the ball. If he is absolutely sure of getting control of the ball, fine. Otherwise, the use of the punch is the safest way to clear it away from the mouth of the goal and out of immediate danger.

After the kick, the goalie should position himself immediately to greater advantage. On a short kick he should come forward cautiously and position himself exactly as he would to play a ball, in play from the field, on that side. He must remember that the opposing forwards behind him are positioned perfectly to play any ball deflected by an overanxious goalie trying to make a play on the short corner kick.

Direct Free Kicks—Check Diagrams 45 through 50.

On all free kicks, the goalie must make sure that the line of defense in front of him is so positioned that if a kick is lobbed over their heads he can make a play on the ball before an opponent can. He must always keep his eye on the ball and position himself in the goal favoring the short side of the angle. He must be aggressive.

Goal Kicks—Check Diagrams 43 and 44.

If he takes the goal kick, one fullback should play in the mouth of the goal. It will be to the team's advantage to have the goalie learn to kick well. If one of the fullbacks takes the kick, the goalie should play in the mouth of the goal, favoring the side from which the kick is being taken. He should be ready for interception by the opponents and a quick break solo or cross.

Indirect Free Kicks—Check Diagrams 51 and 52.

Played the same as direct free kicks. The following indirect free kick situations are played differently than the direct free kick situations: Diagrams 53 through 55.

Touch Line Kicks—Check Diagram 56.

Played the same as a direct free kick. Both on offense and defense, the nearer the goal line the kick is taken, the more the setup is like that of a corner kick.

V

Offensive and Defensive Strategy

OFFENSIVE—DEFENSIVE PATTERNS

No matter what system of attack or play a team uses, it must be developed around the ability of the players, so that as a team every move is sound. For strength is gained through the pooling of the ability of the eleven men rather than on the hope of a few.

Attacks can be broken down into two main categories, the long passing attack and the short passing attack. Although a team might use as its basic pattern of attack a long passing or a short passing game, a good all-around team must blend the two types of attacks to meet the many various problems and situations which have to be met during the course of a season.

The long passing game is a well-organized and well-planned attack based primarily on long accurate passes, each with a definite purpose in mind. It does not mean long aimless kicks, but con-

trolled kicks that are passes which fit into a pattern in getting
the ball up the field the quickest and easiest way to the goal. The
key kick or pass in the long passing game is the first kick. If this
first kick goes astray, one of the big advantages of the long passing
attack, that of getting down the field first with the most, will be
lost. Although in the long passing game the ball is not individually
controlled as much by the players of the attacking team as it is in
the short passing game, this type of game has its distinct advantages. The individual players do not have to be as skilled in
handling the ball in the long passing game as they do in the short
passing game. If they can kick with any degree of accuracy, and
know where they are supposed to kick the ball when they get it,
then they are on their way to developing a reasonably sound long
passing game. Since kicking is one of the fundamentals the beginner first learns, and since it, of all the fundamentals, seems to be
the most natural for him to do, the beginner will adapt himself
easier and more effectively to the long passing game than he will
to the short passing game. The long passing game has the distinct advantage of getting the ball down the field with the minimum amount of ball handling and passing. It gets the ball down
the field often before the defending team has a chance to get organized. Two long accurate passes can carry the ball the length of
the field and change the situation of a team about ready to be
scored on to a team itself in scoring position. A typical long passing game pattern is a kick from a fullback to a wing forward at a
spot diagonally down the field in the penalty box, out of the
goalie's reach, set up for the other wing to make a play on the ball
for a possible score, as in Diagram 9.

The advantages of the long passing attack are negligible when
playing into a strong wind or strong cross wind. Into a strong
wind, both accuracy and distance will be lost. A ball kicked into
the wind will sail high and lose most of its power and distance,
hence, in this situation, the short passing game is more effective.
However, in wet weather, a long passing game is more effective
than the short passing game, since in wet weather the ball is more

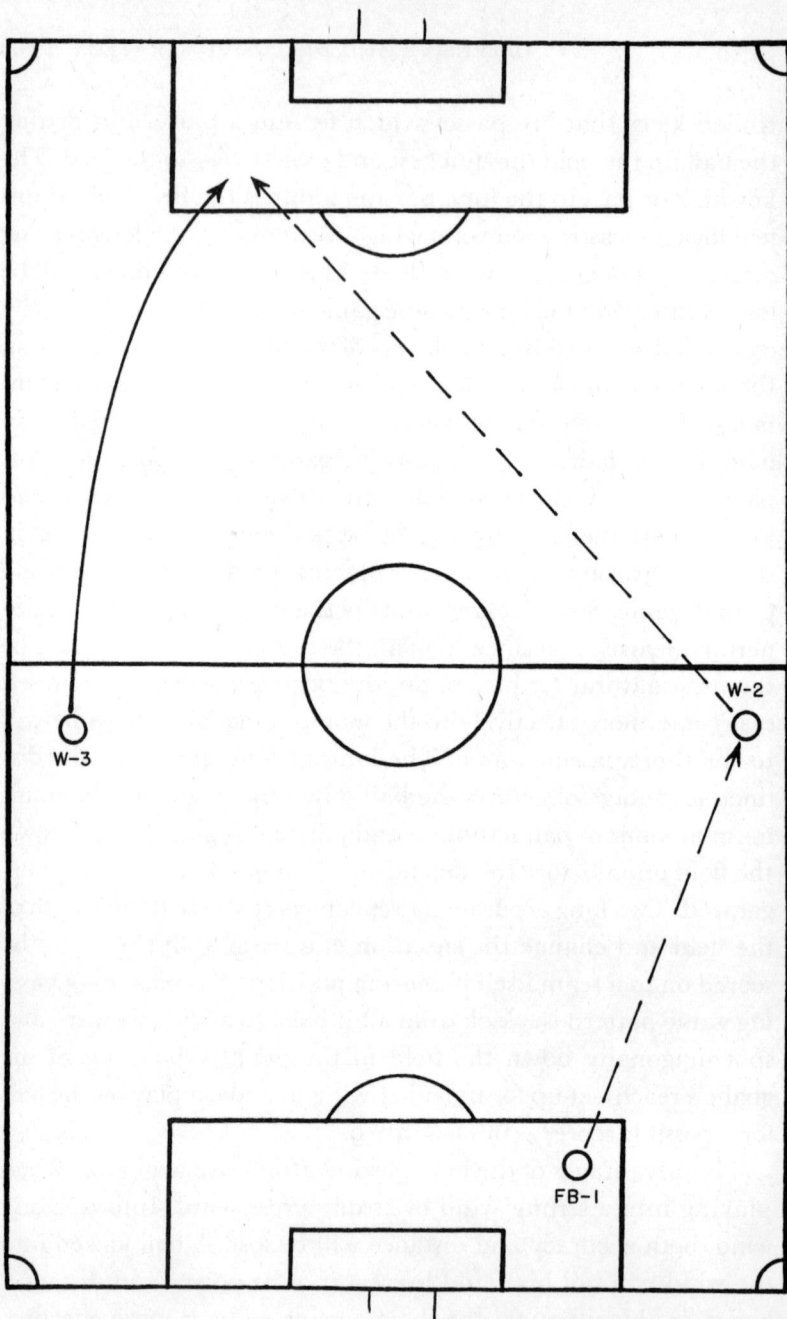

DIAGRAM 9

A TYPICAL LONG PASSING
ATTACK PATTERN

difficult to control and pass, and the short passing game is based primarily on the players' being able to control the ball with short passes on the ground.

The short passing attack demands a good deal of individual brilliance on the part of each member of the offensive team in controlling and handling the ball and in bringing it up the field for scoring opportunities with the use of short passes blended into well-planned combination patterns. This type of attack is more prevalent with the more experienced and skilled players because of the necessity for each player to be able to control the ball through the use of fundamentals and tricks of his own acquired through practice and playing.

No matter what attack is used, there are basic principles that must be incorporated into all offensive plans. One of the most important principles concerns the proper positioning of the players on the field, with and without the ball. Every man on the field must, in every situation, be responsible for covering a certain area and for positioning himself in a spot that will give his team the greatest advantage. No two men must cover the same area because in doing so they make themselves vulnerable in another area. A rule of thumb in this regard is that it should be considered a waste of manpower to have two men in an area that can be covered by one. Furthermore, if this situation exists, one of the players is out of position on the field. One of the most-used basic positioning patterns is the W formation.

The W formation in Diagram 10 shows the relative positions of the forwards to each other on the field. The W formation is very flexible and can be shallow, deep or at times illegible, depending upon the conditions that exist. A long passing game calls for a deep W formation while a short passing game calls for a more shallow W. As a rule, this relation of the forwards to each other exists, and with it many passing patterns can be worked out. Having the players on a soccer team distributed in the best relative positions to each other and to the ball, whether they have the ball or not, is as important a factor in winning a soccer game

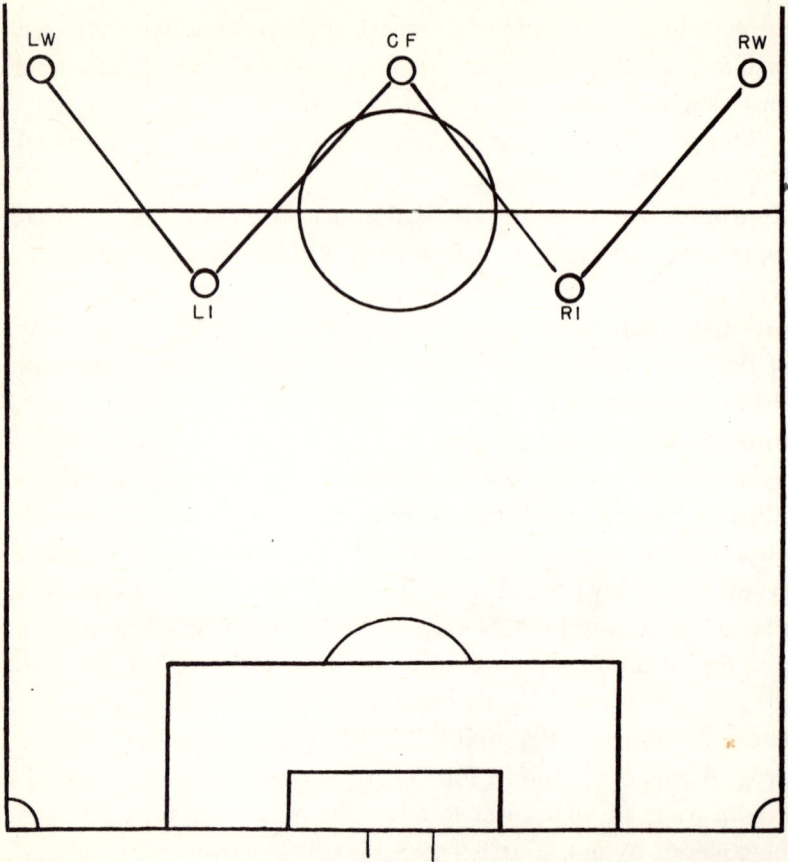

DIAGRAM 10   BASIC RELATIONS OF FORWARDS TO
EACH OTHER IN POSITIONING
THEMSELVES ON THE FIELD TO BE
MOST EFFECTIVE

as it is for the members of a baseball team to cover certain areas on a baseball field. In baseball, the players position themselves to each other to cover the most ground where the ball is most likely to go. They fade off of weaknesses to pack strength in places where, in their judgment, they think it will do them the most good.

In soccer then, each man must play in relatively the same po-

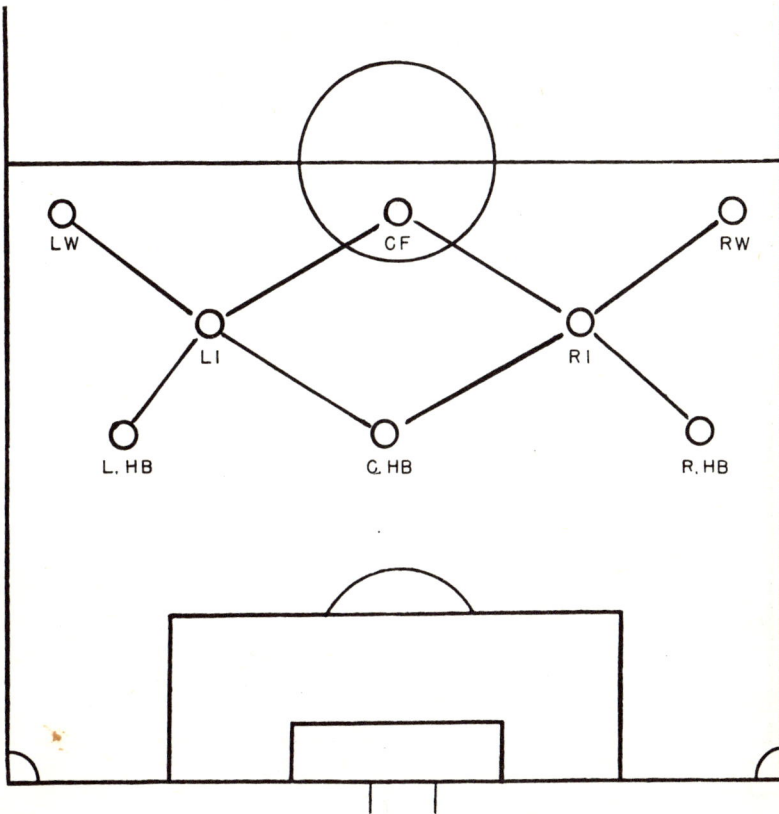

DIAGRAM 11   BASIC RELATION OF FORWARDS AND
HALFBACKS TO EACH OTHER IN
POSITIONING THEMSELVES ON THE
FIELD TO BE MOST EFFECTIVE

sition to the others, but the exact position is determined by the
position of the ball and the strength and weaknesses of the opponents and members of his own team. As stated above, the relative
position of the forwards to each other is the W formation. All
members of the team must have this W formation picture well
creased on their minds so that on defense all areas for passes and
all possible lanes to the goal will be covered, and on the offense
passes can be made to spots and to each other almost blindfolded.
Diagrams 11 and 12 show the relative positions of the halfbacks,

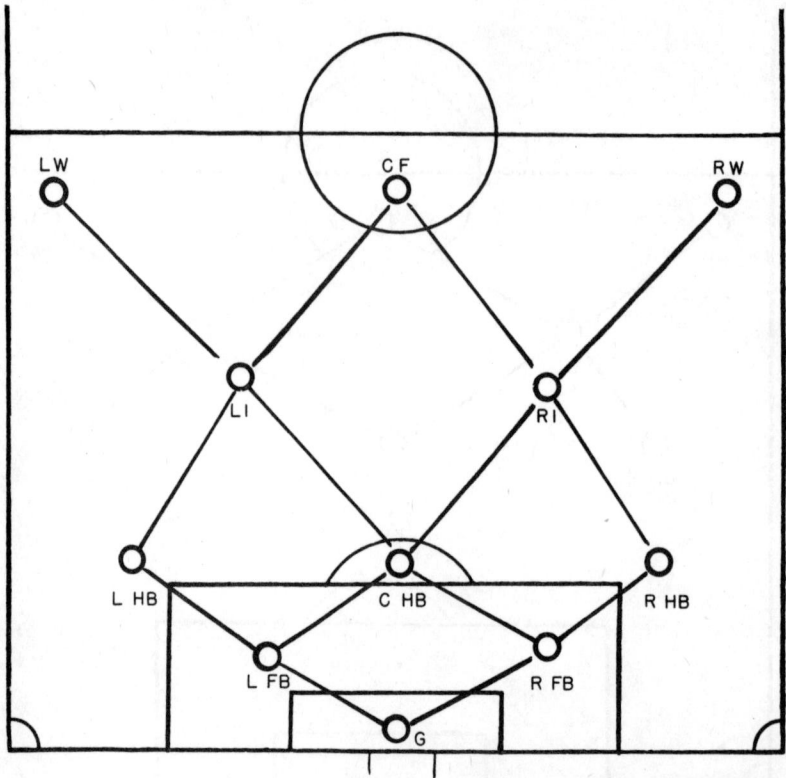

DIAGRAM 12   BASIC RELATION OF FORWARDS,
HALFBACKS AND FULLBACKS TO EACH
OTHER IN POSITIONING THEMSELVES
ON THE FIELD TO BE MOST EFFECTIVE

fullbacks, and forwards to each other. Every line in Diagram 12 presents a passing possibility. Any two or three men can combine in working the ball down the field and through the defense.

There are, however, groups or combinations that are more naturally set up to work together as units than others, only, however, as a part of the whole team picture. For example, the left wing, left inside and left halfback work well as a group as does their counterpart, the right wing forward, right inside, and right halfback. So do the two insides and the center forward, also the center halfback, center forward and either inside. As you can see, each group forms a triangle and offers many opportunities to form combination passing patterns.

All offenses must be flexible enough so that when a player goes out of what is considered his normal position, one of his teammates will switch to the position he left to give the basic pattern the proper balance. This is called switching positions and adds greatly to the possibilities in the offense. Check Diagrams 29, 30 and 30A. A team that does not have variety in its attack and does the same thing over and over again in the same unimaginative way is bound to be stopped cold. Switching fosters initiative and imagination and with it a sound, well-thought-out offense with enough variety to contend with any defensive setup.

All members of the team must have a thorough knowledge of the game and especially know what to do with the ball when they get it. Each member should know the possibilities in every situation and have a clear understanding of what each of his teammates is trying to do. Every team's offense must be so well planned that for every defensive situation it meets, it has a counteroffensive move. The naïve faith that coaches have put into the saying that the best defense is a good offense, has meant grief to many potentially good teams. A defense should not have to depend on the offense for its success; true, if a team can control the ball and keep the pressure on the opponents, it makes the defense look good in a rather negative sort of way. Let us take an arbitrary percentage figure and say that each team evenly matched controls the ball about 50 per cent of the time. I say evenly matched because a team you obviously outclass should not be on your schedule. In this hypothetical case then, if you control the ball 50 per cent of the time, what about the other 50 per cent? Obviously in this 50 per cent the team is only as good as its defense. There certainly is no argument against having a good offense, but it doesn't make your defense and it does not win the close games for you. If the saying said the combination of a good offense and a good defense makes a good team, then it would make more sense.

The offense always seems to have more glamour and appeal to the players than the defense, hence, the coach will have to work harder to stimulate the player's interest in this phase of the game. The defense must have a definite pattern worked out through intelligent study. Every man on the team must understand where every other man fits into the defensive pattern. They must understand that defense is a team effort and that the proper positioning of each man to each other and to the ball results in greater defensive strength. Each man also must be able to size up his own individual defensive problems. In sizing up his own situation, he should know how much and what kind of attention he must give his man. He must find out quickly the opponent's individual strength and the team's offensive patterns and strengths. With this as a necessary preliminary, fading off of the opponent's weaknesses and packing against their strength can be initiated.

Regardless of what the defensive assignments are, the individual assignments must be flexible enough for a back to be able to switch and know that a teammate is falling in behind him to back him up and give the defense its proper balance. For example, a simple and sound switch occurs when the fullback, who normally covers the inside, goes out to cover the wing forward who has got the jump on his own defensive man, the wing halfback. This switch happens often and is very sound since it gives the halfbacks the chance to take advantage of any offensive openings for going in themselves for shots which often on a quick accurate clearing kick by the opponents to the wing forward, finds the wing halfback out of position to assume his original defensive assignment. Furthermore, most insides have the responsibility of covering the halfbacks on defense, and the halfbacks will be in a better position to cover the insides in this situation. This switch makes it possible to nip any offensive thrust in the bud and gives the halfbacks a chance to play a bigger part in the offense without basically weakening the defense, that is, the halfbacks make their offensive moves judiciously. If it isn't possible to nip the offensive thrust early, the fullback does the next best thing: delay, and

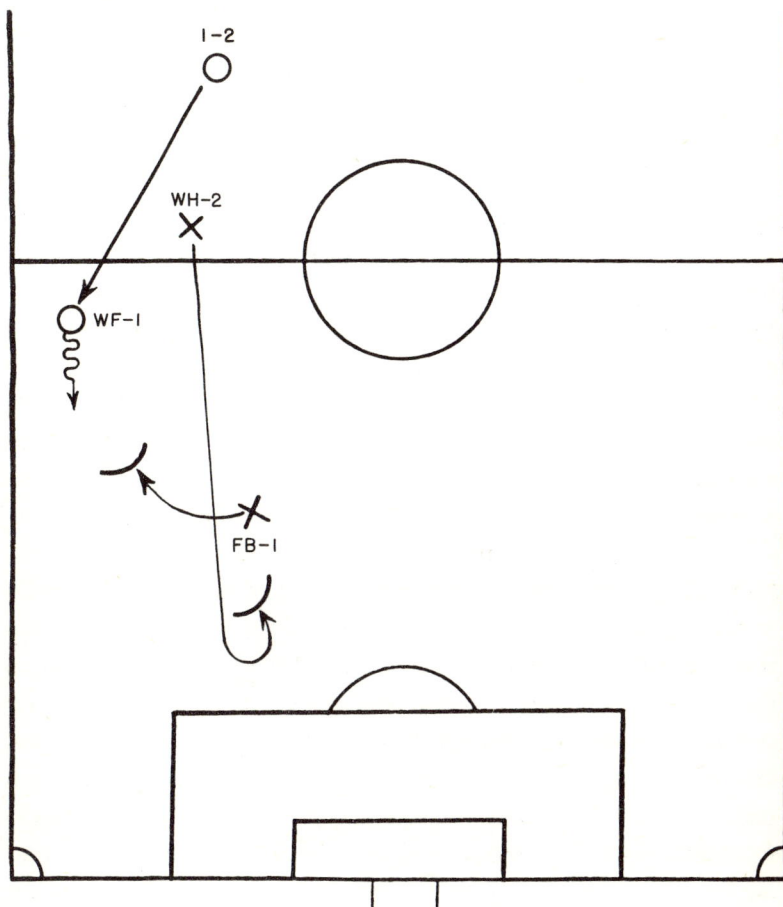

DIAGRAM 13   WING HALFBACK AND FULLBACK
SWITCH ON DEFENSE

*The ball is cleared to the wing forward O1, who has the jump on the wing
halfback X2, teammate of fullback X1, who sizes up the situation immediately and goes over to pick up wing forward O1. Wing halfback X2 drops in
behind X1 to back him up. He should also be ready to cover the inside O2, or
to pick up wing forward O1 if he gets by fullback X1. In that case the fullback drops behind to cover for the halfback X2. This cycle can repeat itself until the offensive thrust is broken up.*

drive the wing to the touch line deep in the corner. The half-back always falls in behind the fullback. For the fullback to drive the wing forward to the touch line, he always plays square off the inside shoulder and ahead of the man with the ball so as not to give him the chance of driving into the middle.

There are other defensive switches which can save players much energy and make a much sounder defense than playing a rigid defensive game of being responsible for only one man. No matter what switches are made, however, there must be a definite understanding between the players. With the roaming or offensive-minded center halfback, the fullbacks must have an understanding in covering the opponent's center forward since on a long clear, the center halfback would many times be caught out of position to cover the center forward.

The reverse of the wing halfback and fullback switch as described above also will nip an opponent's offensive thrust in the bud and give the defensive team possession of the ball up the field, and the possible start of their own offensive thrust. In this switch the wing halfback makes the first move by covering the inside up the field. In this case the fullback does not immediately drive out to cover the wing forward but moves out slowly and cautiously, giving the wing forward a little more freedom of movement than usual. If a pass is made to the wing forward by the inside, the fullback then drives out and covers the wing forward. The fullback, in assuming his position, should also be thinking in terms of intercepting the pass from the inside to the wing forward. This strategy is to encourage the pass to the wing toward the touch line and away from the mouth of the goal, and also to keep the middle of the field defensively packed, ready to cover the inside if he does get by the wing halfback who has done the covering up the field.

These switches are very simple as long as everybody on the team has a thorough knowledge of what is going on and what his job is. The fullback on whose side of the field the ball is, should make the initial move on the switch, followed immediately and automatically by the halfback he is switching with. Every time

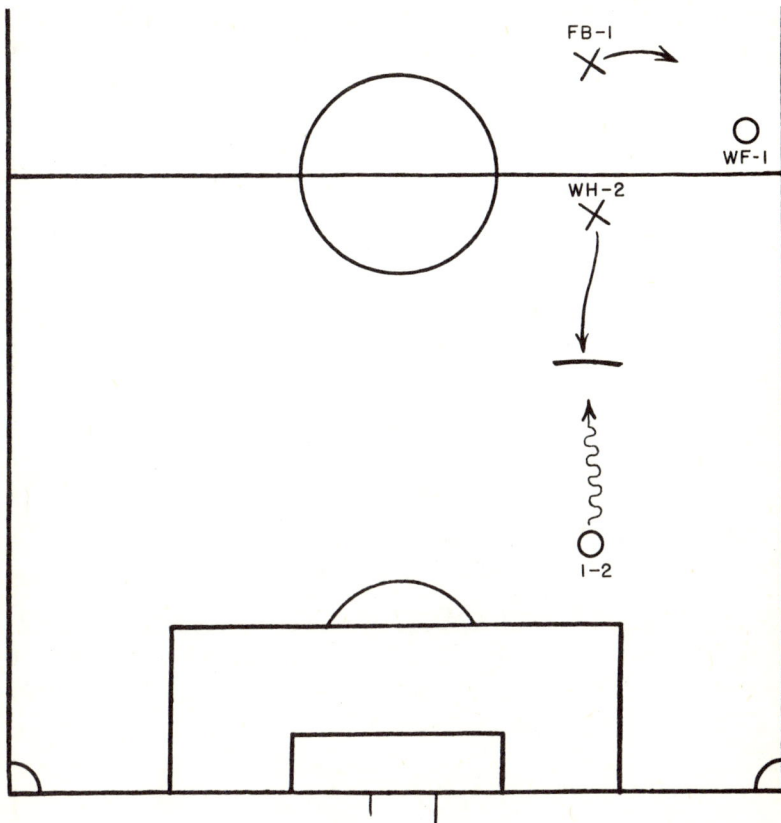

DIAGRAM 14   WING HALFBACK SWITCHING ON
DEFENSE WITH FULLBACK COVERING
INSIDE UP THE FIELD

Inside O2 picks up clearing kick and heads down field. Wing halfback X2 immediately picks up inside O2. Fullback X1 assumes position as described in text.

one fullback goes out to cover the wing forward, the other fullback must move over into the middle to make sure the center forward is covered. Such flexibility and switching in the defense gives strength to the defense and indirectly to the offense.

The only forwards who have any definite defensive assignments are the insides and their job is to cover the three half backs. The **center halfback (the roaming center halfback) is always covered,**

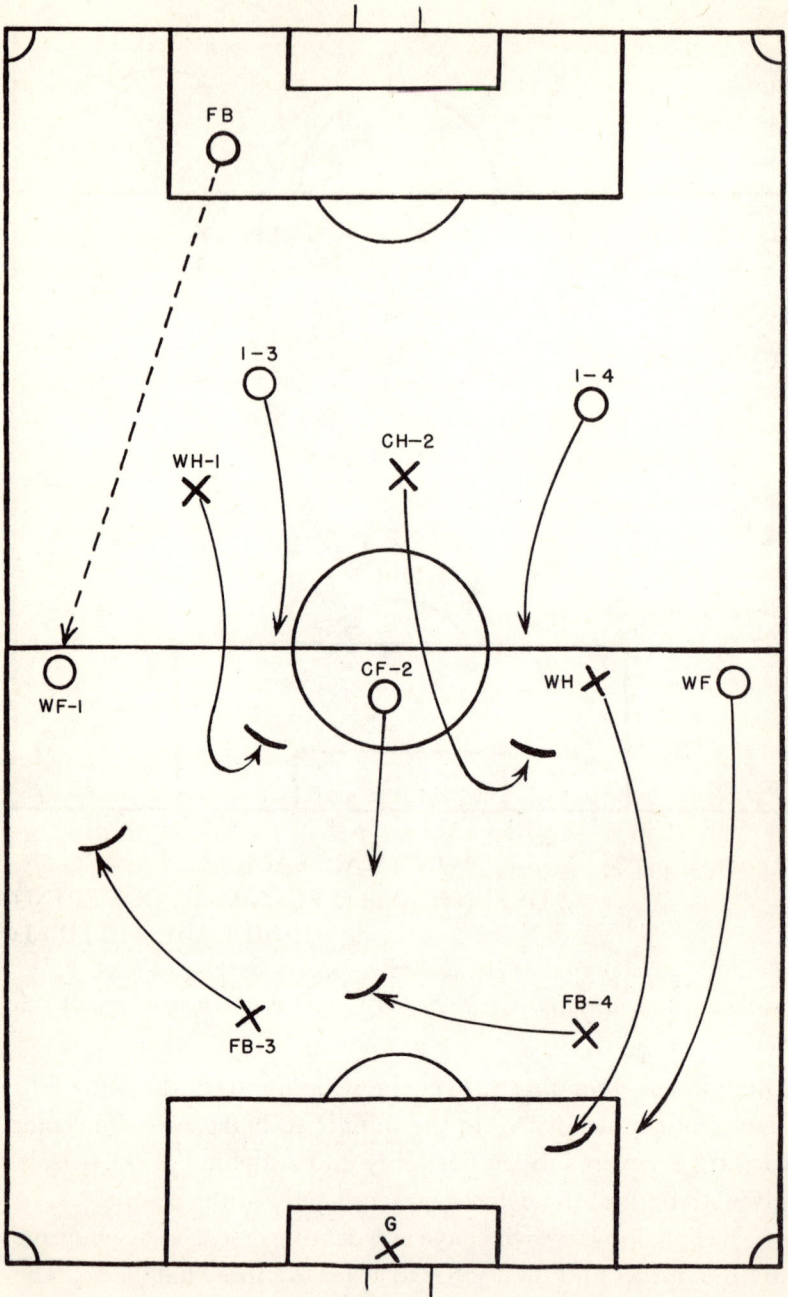

and the wing halfback is covered when the ball is on his side of the field. The other wing halfback is left unguarded until the ball is kicked to his side of the field; then the insides slide over. The inside covering the center halfback slides over to cover the wing halfback, and the inside covering the wing halfback slides over and picks up the center halfback. It is quite important for the insides to size up the opponent's halfbacks quickly and decide how much defensive attention they are going to need and then take their liberties. On defense, it is best to start off cautiously, size up the situation, and then take liberties by fading off to help teammates if they need it.

The insides must realize that they are a definite part of the offense and must not play so that they are making the opposing halfbacks offensive rather than defensive players. They must, as part of their strategy, keep the halfbacks defensive minded. If the insides find that the halfbacks never go in to take a shot or do not go up very far to back the forwards on offense, then they should play them loosely and position themselves to control the clearing kicks.

Insides should be very conscious of halfbacks dribbling the ball up the field to draw a man or to cross. If there is any spot where the halfbacks are very much open it is in the middle third of the field. The insides can stop many halfbacks who get dribble happy when they see an open field in front of them.

A well-planned defense will always have the individual players so distributed that the defensive man playing the ball will always be backed up by one of his own teammates. The exception, of

---

DIAGRAM 15   DOUBLE SWITCH ON DEFENSE WITH BOTH FULLBACKS INVOLVED

Fullback X3 picks up X1's (wing halfback) man, who received the clearing kick. Fullback X4 drifts over into the middle to pick up center forward O2, who is center halfback's (X2) man. Halfbacks X1 and X2 pick up the insides O3 and O4 who were originally assigned to fullbacks X3 and X4.

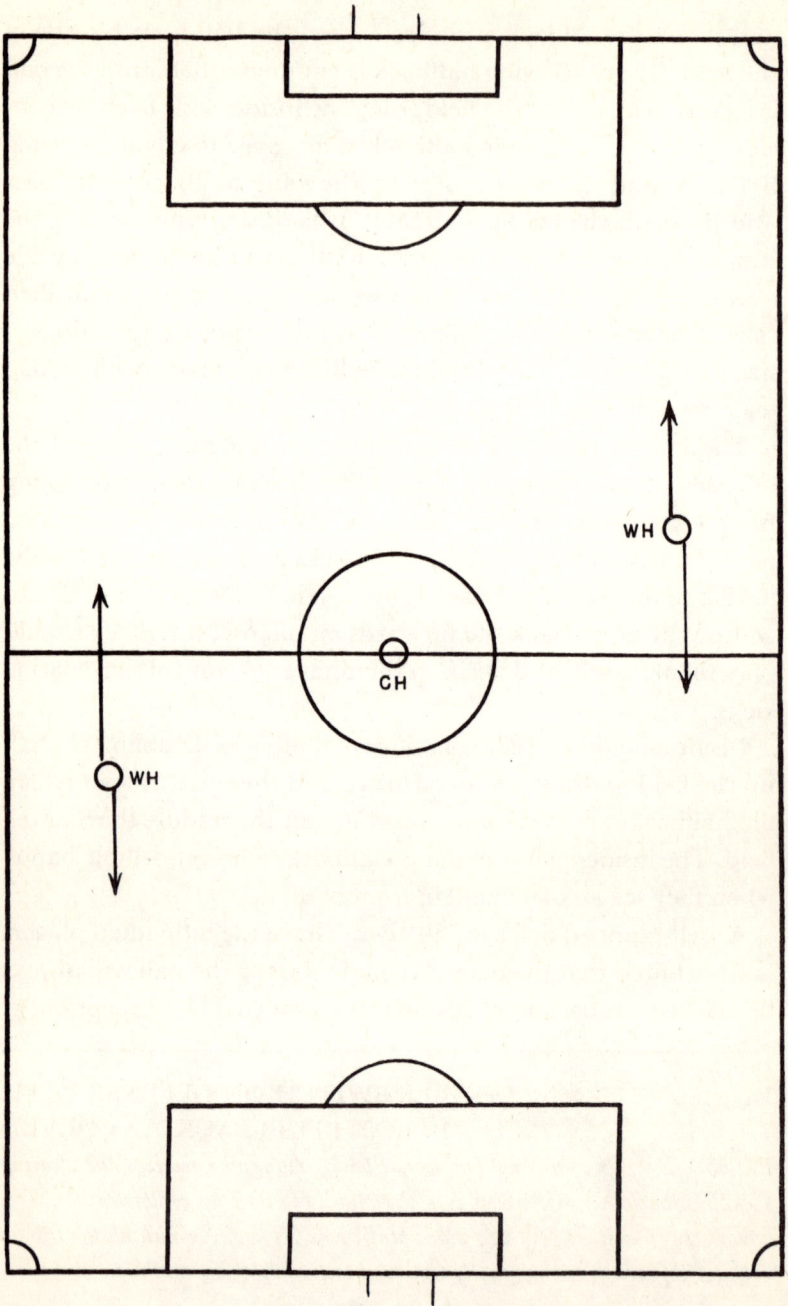

course, to this rule is the goalie, so if you can't give him support, don't get in his way.

The wing halfbacks position themselves by pivoting around the center halfback.

The area in front of the goal, the middle of the field, should always be covered. If one fullback goes out to cover a wing forward, the other positions himself in the middle to intercept passes and crosses, and to cover any man coming down the middle. The wing halfback backs up the fullback in the middle.

The defense must be very much aware of plays to decoy the defensive men out of position and thus to open up the middle for the insides or wing forwards to get in for good shots in front of the goal. A well-planned and well-organized defense will find the players falling into the strongest defensive pattern to meet any situation almost intuitively.

Two other defenses are the third-man-back and the zone defense. In the third-man-back defense, the center halfback shadows the center forward and always plays within covering distance of the man. Obviously, the center halfback has one job: to stop the center forward; this means his job is strictly defense as compared to the more offensive-minded center halfback in the roaming type game.

In the zone defense, players are placed to cover certain areas in the penalty box or close to it.

DIAGRAM 16   WING HALFBACKS POSITION THEMSELVES
BY PIVOTING AROUND THE CENTER
HALFBACK

The positioning and pivoting of the wing halfbacks around the center halfback distributes offensive and defensive support where and when it is needed most. The wing halfback up the field with the ball will be supporting his wing forward and inside in pressing the attack. The wing halfback on the other side of the field will be in the best position possible to pick up any clearing cross kicks, and hence, keep the pressure on the opponents by constantly feeding the forwards. The relative positions and moves are always the same, but the exact moves and positions depend on the situation as it exists.

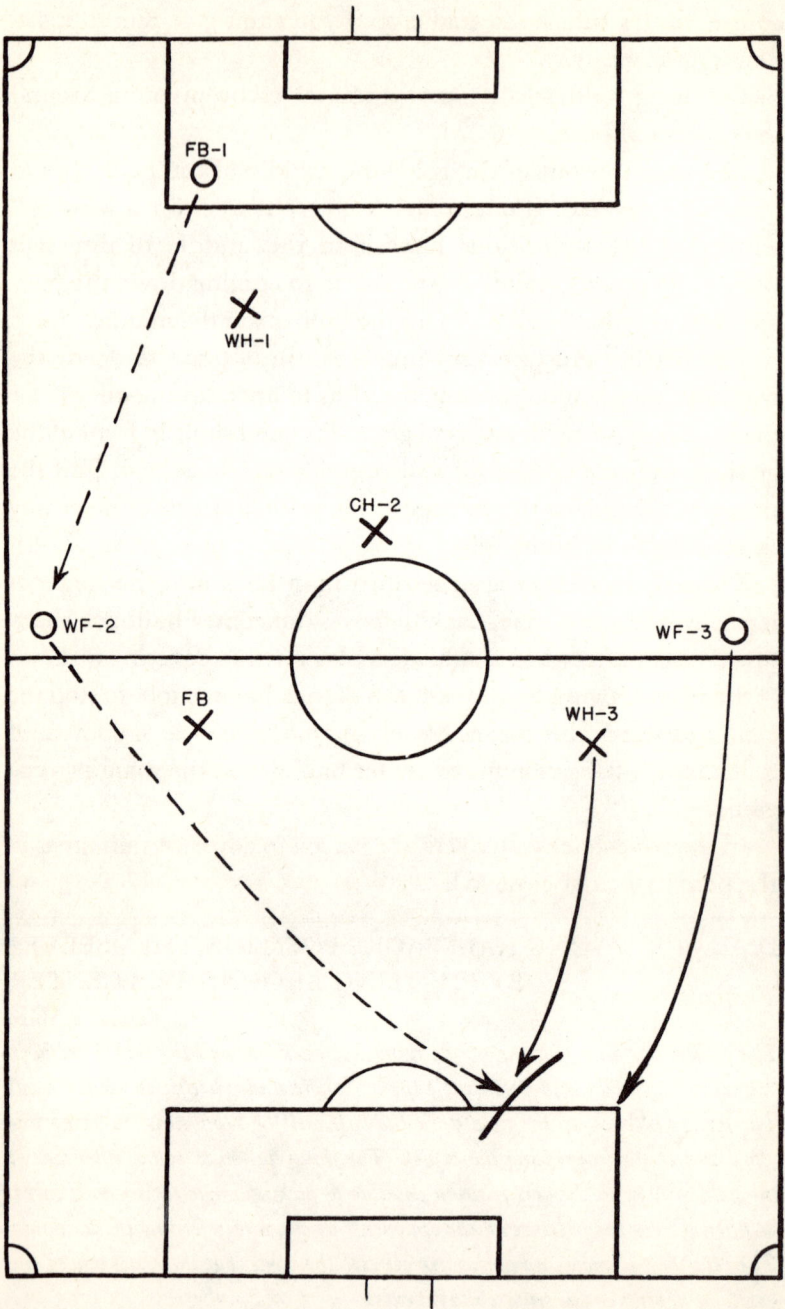

The ways to beat a zone defense are to get down the field before the defense can be set up and organized; wing forwards can dribble in, draw the fullback out and then pass into a man who cuts into the area left open by the fullback—a cross pass to wing forward cutting on other side in behind the defense.

UNCONTROLLABLE FACTORS TO CONSIDER IN PLANNING GAME STRATEGY

There are some factors which the players have no control over, which many times decide the eventual outcome of a game. These uncontrollable factors come under the heading of elements, of which rain, wind, snow and sun are the main components. In playing a wet ball on a wet field, the long passing game is more effective than the short passing game since the wet ball is so much more difficult to handle. A ball on a wet field does not bounce but slides and comes off the ground much lower and faster than a bouncing ball on a dry field.

Hard passes into the area of the mouth of the goal often end in the goal because of the difficulty the goalie has in handling the ball. There are more rebounds off of the goalie in wet weather since the ball is so much harder to handle. The offensive team with the ball around the mouth of the goal should be driving hard for the rebounds off the goalie, and should also be ready to pick up and take advantage of poor clearing kicks by the backs. In wet weather, any shot to either side of the goalie will be a much more difficult save for the goalie because of the goalie's poor footing,

---

DIAGRAM 17   WING HALFBACKS ALWAYS DROP BACK AND POSITION THEMSELVES TO INTERCEPT CROSSES WHEN THE BALL IS CLEARED OR IS BEING BROUGHT DOWN THE OPPOSITE SIDE OF THE FIELD

Fullback O1 clears to wing forward O2. When pass is being made, wing halfback X3 drops back into position as indicated in diagram to intercept any possible cross kicks to wing forward O3.

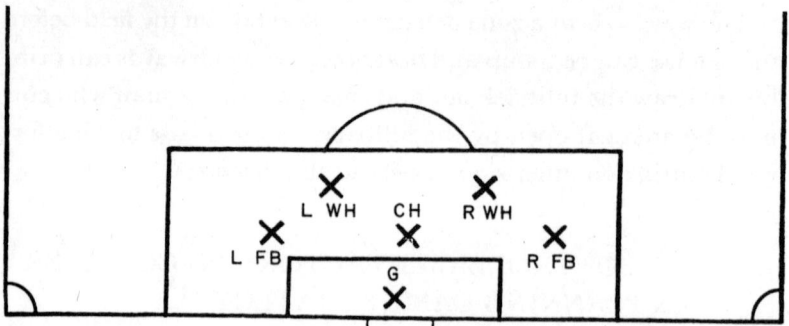

DIAGRAM 18   TYPICAL ZONE DEFENSE SETUP WITH
EACH MAN ASSIGNED TO COVER AN AREA
IN FRONT OF THE GOAL

The zone defense is set up in front of the mouth of the goal in the penalty box. In other areas the man-to-man defense is used. The positions of the men are determined by the position of the ball. The object is to keep the lane between the ball and the goal padded. It can definitely be used to stop any center forward or inside men who outclass the defensive backs.

plus the conditions ideal for poor ball handling. With that in mind, shots should be kept on the ground to either side of the goalie. A shot in wet weather doesn't have to just skin the goalpost or be shot like a rocket to get into the goal. Wet weather definitely favors the shooters.

The wind is another strong factor in deciding the outcome of many games. The decision as to whether to take the wind as an ally the first quarter and not have it the last will always be a source of argument. I happen to be one of the group (and I don't know how big) who believes that a bird in the hand is worth two in the bush, hence, take the wind as an ally while it is around. Further, the wind can be the factor which gives a team a couple of quick goals and a decided psychological edge. A team ahead by a couple of goals can almost dictate the type of game played. It will give a team the confidence it needs to relax and play heads-up, smart soccer all the way.

On the other hand, for the team scored upon it can be the psychological factor which will cause the bottom of their entire offense and defense to fall apart. A couple of quick goals against any team will affect their physical efforts. There will be a tendency to divert from their regular steady game, resulting in more errors and inevitably, wide-open breaks for the other team.

In playing into the wind, a short passing attack is the better game; while playing with the wind, long low accurate kicks will bring better results. With the wind as an ally, a shallow, up-the-field, just on-side W formation is pertinent, while on the other hand, when driving into the wind, a deep W is a sounder setup. On a cross wind, the ball must be played low into the wind or on the ground. The ball should be brought down on both sides of the field, if possible, yet, with a cross wind, it is better to have the key kick set up so that the wind is behind the ball.

The sun can play a definite part in the outcome of a game, especially if it affects the vision of the goalie. If the sun is a factor, it should be considered wisely in the choice of goals at the beginning of the game.

Although it doesn't come under the heading of an element, the spin on the ball is a difficult factor to contend with from the receiver's point of view, and many balls are lost because the pass receiver does not know how to judge the spin. The spin on the ball has much to do with the direction of the flight of the ball in the air and after the bounce. Any ball kicked to either side of the vertical axis of the ball will curve sideways and have a spin going around the vertical axis. On the bounce, the ball will bounce to one side or the other of a player standing directly in line with the flight of the ball. Oftentimes a player learns to handle this type of ball well by playing it on the fly or immediately after it hits and leaves the ground. It is better to drive into these kicks and play the ball before it plays you.

Any ball hit below or above the horizontal axis will have a top or back spin. Neither is too hard to handle as long as the player gets in direct line with the ball and uses his body as a safety valve. Practice will make a ball with a spin relatively easy to handle.

Another factor which has to be considered but does not come

under the heading of elements is the type and condition of the field. The condition of the field will have much to do with the type of passes and shots the players use and will have a definite effect on the way they handle the ball. If the field is smooth and well-turfed, it will be slower than a skin field. If the field is rocky and rough, the short passing type of game will be affected more than the long passing game.

DROP BALL SITUATION

The drop ball situation is used by an official to put the ball back into play after time has been temporarily suspended for some reason other than those covered in the rules. To put the ball back into play, the official drops the ball to the ground in between two opposing players. The ball must touch the ground before a play can be made on it by any player. A goal may be scored direct.

The drop ball situation comes up in a game very seldom, hence, very little time should be devoted to it. However, there are two places on the field where this situation could result in a score, hence, a team must know how best to set up in each situation. If the kick is taken directly in front of the defending team's goal, the ball should be played by the defending player exactly as when making a head-on tackle: The leg should be extended forward, trapping the ball with the inside of the foot or the sole of the foot. This will momentarily stop the forward progress of the ball and may offer the player the possibility of getting possession and clearing the ball immediately away from the mouth of the goal. Playing the ball this way avoids a rebound directly at the goal and might offer a good possibility of the opponent's kicking the ball hard against the inside of the defender's foot and away from the mouth of the goal. The players on the team with their backs against the goal should guard their men closely, stay between their men and the goal, and drive hard for the ball after the initial play in an attempt to make the clear. The goalie should position himself in the goal as he would playing a shot from the field from that point.

When the ball is taken directly in front of the opponent's goal, the first thought for the person playing the ball and shooting at the goal is to do everything possible to get control of it, to shoot or to pass it off to a teammate in a better position to shoot. If the player cannot get possession of the ball, he should do everything possible to keep it in around the mouth of the goal and prevent the opponents from clearing it. Again, rather than taking a wild swing at the ball, it is much wiser to play the ball the same as when it is in front of the player's own goal. The rest of the team should play in a position for a pass, or be ready to play the rebound as an excellent scoring chance. The players, shooting for the goal in front of where the drop ball situation occurs, should be alert and driving, should not bunch, and should try to open the defense so that it will be easier to drive in for a pass or to play any rebound.

STRATEGY BASED ON WHAT YOU KNOW OF YOUR OPPONENT AND THE ELEMENTS

Game strategy should be based on the analysis of the opponent's team and individual strengths and weaknesses as compared to your own strengths and weaknesses. Sound strategy is simply aimed at having your offensive strength hit the opponent's defensive weaknesses, and to pack your defense to meet their offensive strengths. Some of the questions that must be considered in planning game strategy are:

Q. What sort of an offensive pattern or patterns do the opponents use? Long passing? Short passing?

A. If the opponents play a long passing game, have your defense with the forwards playing a deeper W formation. The halfbacks on the weak side (side opposite to where the ball is) should play deeper and be ready to intercept any crosses. The halfback on the strong side should play up and try to stop or at least interfere with the opponent's getting off a good accurate long kick.

The fullbacks should play the same as the wing halfbacks.

If the opponents play a short passing game, set your defense with the forwards playing a shallow W formation. Also play closer to your men and try to stop the attack up the field.

Q. Do they have any special way of bringing the ball down the field? Do they always bring the ball down the same way, on the same side of the field, or do they have variety in their offense?

A. Obviously, if you do not know their offensive patterns, set up a cautious or conservative defense until you analyze them. Once their patterns are analyzed, set up to pack against their strength and take full advantage of their weaknesses.

Q. Is there any one player who brings the ball down more than another?

A. If so, give him special attention by either putting your best man on him who should then be instructed to play him closely, or double-team the outstanding player.

Q. Where is their strength on offense—down the middle or coming in from the sides?

A. Pack your defense to meet their offensive pattern strengths by taking advantage or sagging off of their offensive pattern weaknesses.

Q. Have they any particular combination play or plays that have been setting up their scoring opportunities?

A. Pack your defense to meet their offensive pattern strengths by taking advantage or sagging off of their offensive pattern weaknesses.

Q. Are the players on the opposing team small and fast or big and slow?

A. If the opponents are small and fast, the halfback on the weak side will have to play deeper on defense to intercept clearing kicks so as not to let the opposing forwards get the ball and set up a three forwards on two fullbacks situation. If the wing on the weak side of the field does pick up the clearing kick, the halfback should set up to tackle, or delay the attack by driving the wing forward toward the touch line and deep into the corner with the ball. He should keep the wing forward with the ball away from the mouth of the goal and further, stop him from getting off a good pass or cross. He should not let the forwards get the ball behind the defense if he can prevent it. If the opponents are slow and big, the halfbacks should try to get the ball down the field as fast as they can, and try to clear the fullbacks so that the forwards just on-side can drive in for free balls kicked over the heads of the defense.

Q. Are their fullbacks taller than your forwards?

A. If so, the ball should be played on the ground around the mouth of the goal rather than being played with high lobs, which, obviously, is to the advantage of the taller players.

Q. Have they been doing all their scoring in the first period or half and then pulling into their shell?

A. This is a psychological factor more than a deciding factor in setting up the offense or defense. Psychologically, it makes a difference in the frame of mind of a team to know that it has held a heretofore high-scoring-first-half team to no goals during this period. It obviously will have a pressing effect on the team held scoreless.

Q. Are they a front running team—do they fall apart once they fall behind?

A. Psychological factor again. However, it might be well to set up and be ready with the defense to stop any immediate offensive thrusts. Set up your defense with this in mind, but do not hesitate to take advantage of any offensive breaks.

Q. How have they been scored on? Are there any glaring weaknesses in their defense?

A. If you know their defensive weaknesses hit them early. An early score will immediately put the pressure on the opponents and with it more breaks for your team.

Q. If the fullbacks cover the wing forwards, who covers the middle on a quick break?

A. If the fullbacks cover the wing forwards and leave the middle open, obviously, come down the middle. If the fullbacks cover the middle and leave the wing forwards open, the play should be to draw and pass off to the wing forward that is open. If one fullback goes out to meet the wing forward coming down with the ball and the other fullback covers the middle, a lead cross to the wing forward on the other side of the field is in order. Simply play the wing forwards if the middle is covered, and play the middle if the fullbacks play the wing forwards.

Q. Defensively, are the opponents weaker on one side of the field than the other?

A. Obviously hit the weak side.

Q. Who covers the halfbacks on defense, if anybody?

A. If the halfbacks are left open, uncovered, they should dribble in for shots from just outside of the penalty box. If the insides come back to cover the halfbacks, keep them up there by intercepting clearing kicks and going in for an occasional shot. If you can make defensive men out of the opposing insides, you obviously have weakened the opponent's offense.

Q. On defense, do they play the third-man-back game or do they play the roaming center halfback offensive type of game?

A. If they play the third-man-back game, more than likely the center forward will be closely watched which means clearing kicks should be made to the wing forwards and the ball should be brought down the side. Also the center forward should set himself up occasionally as a decoy by moving out of the center and taking his defensive man out of the center. This move will open up the center of the field for a teammate to drive in for a spot-lead pass. Also the center forward should switch with his teammates by bringing the ball down occasionally in the wing forward position.

Playing against the roaming center halfback game, the center forward will find himself open more often and occasionally will enjoy a perfect solo drive situation. Also many times this defense will present a three-on-two situation which calls for the dribble, draw, pass-off and cut for a repass pattern.

Q. Do they have a man who can kick a long goal kick and do they have any purpose and accuracy in the kick?

A. Analyze and set defense to meet the situation.

Q. When they take a goal kick do the wing forwards play up and then drive down toward the goal they are shooting at to pick up long accurate kicks, or do the wing forwards play dead and stand and wait?

A. If the wing forwards are driving towards their own goal to pick up the ball kicked ahead of them, the wing halfbacks should play down the field in a more favorable position ready to intercept. By all means the wing halfbacks should not play alongside of the wing forwards on the kick and have the wing forwards outdrive them down the field to get possession of the ball. If the wing forwards play dead, obviously, be aggressive and set yourself up to drive in for the ball and intercept.

Q. Do the opponents have any definite setup on free kicks or do they merely kick in the direction they are shooting?

A. In any event, keep the middle of the field packed in the defensive end by having the wing halfbacks play the wing forwards loosely; when you play loosely and pack the middle, be ready for a kick deep toward the corner for the wing forward to pick up. If your defensive setup does this it is definitely to your advantage. Set up primarily to keep the kick out of the middle of the field and away from the mouth of the goal. If they have any special plays from free kick situations try to pack your defense to stop them.

Q. When the opposing team takes a goal kick, do they cover the wing forwards and insides closely or do they leave one or the other reasonably open?

A. On an interception, play the men who are open.

Q. Do they have any weaknesses in their defense against free kicks? Do they play too far out from the goal or too close to the goal?

A. Elementary to play their weaknesses. If they play too far out, kick over the defense; if they play too deep, play to the side or on the ground to a teammate in front.

Q. Is there any one man on the opposing team that the opponents depend on to do their scoring?

A. Cover him closely with a dependable defensive man or double-team him.

Q. Are there any special strengths or weaknesses of the individual players?

A. If there are, obviously, take advantage of them. For example, fullbacks not being able to head the ball because of size or awkwardness; no switching on defense which gives one or two of your men a better chance to control ball and bring the ball downfield to set up plays.

Q. Can the forwards be tackled or are they clever enough to fake and feint around the defense?

A. If they are clever, play them loosely and switch whenever necessary. Backing each other up on defense is a must.

Q. Are the members of the team as a whole well drilled in their fundamentals or can they be licked by not being able to head a ball well or trap a ball well, etc.?

A. If they aren't well drilled in fundamentals, drive against them on both offense and defense and take the ball away from them. They will be very susceptible to this.

Q. Is the center forward fast and clever enough to get by a back to go in for a solo?

A. If the center forward is clever and fast, first play him very closely so that it is almost impossible for him to get the ball; however, if he does get the ball, play him loosely and have an understanding with the other backs to pick him up if he does get by you. Don't under any circumstances give ground and back into the mouth of the goal. Drive him out to the side, if possible, diagnose his moves as quickly as you can and then set up to meet his strength.

Q. Can and does the center forward shoot with either foot or can he only shoot with one?

A. If he can only hit with one foot, play the shooting foot. If he can shoot with both, then be aware of feints and fakes. Above all, keep your balance.

Q. Does the center forward have any special shooting habits or set pattern that he follows when he gets the ball?

A. Play his strength.

Q. Does the center forward pass off well and does he make the most of his opportunities?

A. Diagnose his pass-off habits and play to intercept. Also drive hard against him to make him pass hurriedly and inaccurately.

Q. Does the center forward usually play just on-side ready for a quick break and ready to drive down to pick up any kicks over the heads of the defense?

A. If he is faster than you are, you must position yourself to offset his advantage of speed. You must have an understanding with your other backs to switch with you on defense and pick up if the opponent does get the jump on you.

Q. Does he head well?

A. If the center forward heads the ball well, you will have to assign a man of good size who can head the ball well to take care of him. This defensive man must be aggressive.

Q. Does he have to trap the ball before getting rid of it?

A. If he has to trap the ball before kicking it, it will give you a little more freedom on defense since you have time to recover and try to take the ball away from the opponent. Drive hard against a man who has difficulty in controlling the ball and try to intercept the ball before the opponent has a chance to get control of it and shoot.

Q. Do their insides cover the halfbacks on defense, and if they do, how far back do they go to cover them?

A. If the insides cover the halfbacks on defense, the halfbacks can make defensive men out of the insides by pressing the attack and going in occasionally for shots. Any time the halfbacks go in for shots, they should have an understanding with the other backs on switching and covering for them on defense. The defense, in any event, should be switched around so that the halfbacks can take advantage of the defensive omissions or commissions of the insides, or whoever covers them.

Q. Do the insides take the 1–2 punch out of their offense by covering the halfbacks unnecessarily close?

A. The insides will be made into defensive men if they play the halfbacks or any other opponent too closely on defense. If the insides do cover closely on defense, the men they cover should keep pressing on offense which undoubtedly affects the insides' offensive usefulness.

Q. When the insides get the ball in the center of the field, do they dribble too much, which gives your defense time to get back to cover?

A. If the insides do dribble too much, it means your halfbacks can take more liberties on offense because of the time element. Also, the halfbacks should tackle the insides up the field to either take the ball away from them or cause them to pass off inaccurately.

Q. When the insides pass off do they pass off any one way, to any one man or spot more than another?

A. If they do the same thing all the time in the same situation, pack your defense to intercept passes or to stop the opponents from setting up so that they can revert to patterns.

Q. Are they eager to get rid of the ball?

A. If the insides are eager to get rid of the ball, try to intercept bad passes by playing them loosely. Passes made hurriedly usually are bad passes. On the other hand, getting rid of the ball hurriedly may be the tip-off that they cannot handle the ball well. Try to find out, by rushing them, which will end up by your getting possession of the ball many times.

Q. Do the insides use their wing forwards and halfbacks well in combination?

A. If the insides do play well in combination with their team-mates, be ready for the pattern of a pass-off to the wing or halfback, a cut towards the goal by the inside and a lead pass over the heads of the defense.

Q. Are the insides an offensive threat or can they be sagged off of so that help can be given another teammate in covering a more dangerous opponent on the defense?

A. Take advantage of every weakness of your opponent to strengthen both your team's offense and defense.

Q. Can they head well enough to be a threat on corner kicks and crosses?

A. If the insides head well, it may be necessary to switch men in certain defensive situations so that a big rugged aggressive player who heads well can check the good heading inside.

Q. Can the wing forwards kick with either foot?

A. If the wing forwards can kick well with either foot, play them head on, do not commit yourself or favor either side, and above all, keep your balance and be aware of feints and fakes. If the wing forwards can kick with only one foot, play off the strong foot. Just remember that every fake a one-footed kicker makes is made to set up the kicking foot.

Q. Are the wing forwards fast and clever?

A. If the wing forwards are clever and fast, do not play them closely or they will show their heels to you. Have an understanding with all backs behind you to be ready to switch. If the kicks to the wing forwards are inaccurate, try to intercept as many kicks to them as you can. Also play more behind the fast, clever wing forwards so they cannot run by you to pick up any lead passes. Set yourself in position once they get the ball to tackle or drive them out to the touch line.

Q. Do the wing forwards go in for shots or are they used exclusively for bringing the ball down and crossing?

A. If the wing forwards go in for shots, tackle as far away from the goal as possible and have an understanding with the fullbacks to pick up in the event the wing forward gets by you. If the wing forwards are used exclusively in bringing the ball down to center or cross, drive them out toward the touch line and deep into the corner. Do everything possible to make your opponents hurry their crosses and lose occuracy which should set up a very possible interception by one of your own teammates.

Q. Have the wing forwards a good cross? Do they get rid of the ball soon or do they carry it down too far into the corner? Where do their crosses usually go?

A. If the wing forwards do have a good cross, the weak-side halfback and fullback must position themselves to intercept. If the wing forwards carry the ball deep into the corner, the chances of a successful cross are diminished.

Q. Do they switch positions often or do they stick religiously to the touch line?

A. If the wing forwards switch positions in setting themselves up or in bringing the ball down the field, the defensive men must be alert and go with them or have a distinct understanding with a teammate to pick up in the event the wing forwards shake themselves free. If the wing forwards stick religiously to the touch line, the defensive job is greatly minimized—defense should keep the wing forwards there, if possible.

Q. Do they play right next to the touch line or do they give themselves room to work between the touch line and the defensive man?

A. If the wing forwards play next to the touch line, they cut their usefulness down considerably, since, obviously, they cut down their working room. If the wing forwards play about six or eight feet inside the touch line, the defensive man's job is greater since the wing forwards have so much more room to work in, and, hence, make more ground for the defensive man to cover.

Q. Do the wing forwards use their halfbacks and do they play well in combination with their insides?

A. Whenever the wing forwards play in combination with the halfbacks and insides, be ready for the pass, cut and lead pass through or over and ahead of the defense pattern.

Q. Are the halfbacks offensive threats?

A. If the halfbacks are offensive threats, obviously, they will have to be checked. If the halfbacks commit themselves on offense more than usual, then the forwards will find themselves free more than usual. In this situation, clearing kicks should be hurried down to your offensive end of the field which will find your teammates usually outnumbering the defense. A long passing game will be effective when playing against offensive-minded halfbacks.

Q. Do the halfbacks play well with the forwards and keep the pressure on by controlling the clearing kicks and putting them back in to the forwards?

A. If the halfbacks do keep pressing the attack by controlling the clearing kicks, then the insides or some other player should be assigned to play the halfbacks closely to intercept or hurry the halfbacks in getting rid of the ball inaccurately, or tackle and take the ball away from them.

Q. Is there any one halfback who would be more apt to go in for a shot than any of the others?

A. If there is one outstanding halfback, then he should be given special defensive attention, that is, a man should be definitely assigned to the offensive-minded halfback. Stop him as far away from his goal as possible and also push your own offense down his side of the field.

Q. Do the wing halfbacks drop back and cover for crosses?

A. If the wing halfbacks do not drop back and cover for crosses, a sharp cross from one wing forward down the field to the other wing forward will prove effective.

Q. Do the halfbacks back each other up well?

A. If the halfbacks do not back up each other well, occasionally an attempt to dribble by a back will prove worthwhile or a lead pass over the heads of the defense will prove effective.

Q. Do the halfbacks commit themselves very much by going way up the field in backing up the forward line so that it leaves the wings wide open for the first clearing pass?

A. Obviously, if the halfbacks do, the clearing kicks should be made to the wing forwards and an attempt should be made to set up immediately a long passing attack pattern.

Q. Do the halfbacks dribble a good deal?

A. If the halfbacks do dribble too much it means more time for you and your teammates to get back on defense, hence, more time to press the offense. Players, usually the insides, should be assigned the job of tackling the halfbacks when they dribble. This will stop the halfbacks from feeding the forwards and putting the ball in play in their offensive end of the field. It will also give the insides a chance to start a quick offensive thrust if they tackle and get possession of the ball.

Q. Can the fullbacks kick with either foot or is either one or both one-footed kickers?

A. If the fullbacks can kick well with only one foot, rush hard so that they cannot set up for a kick with the better kicking foot.

Q. Do the fullbacks play the wing forwards or the insides? If the fullbacks play the wing forwards, does that leave the middle of the field wide open?

A. On defense, if the fullbacks play the opposing wing forwards and leave the middle open, hit the middle.

Q. Do the fullbacks play in tandem or parallel?

A. If the fullbacks play parallel, long lead passes over their heads with the forwards driving down to pick the ball up will certainly be effective. Use the long passing game when faced with this fullback setup.

Q. Do the fullbacks play near the middle of the field or lay back when the ball is in the other end of the field?

A. If the fullbacks play near the middle of the field, use the long passing game. If they lay back deep, then the forwards should be picking up the clearing kicks around the middle of the field. They should then set up the dribble, draw, pass off and cut for repass pattern.

Q. Do the fullbacks come out and tackle immediately or do they back and give ground to the forwards driving in? When the fullbacks tackle, do they do it wisely or do they drive out without caution or any consideration of the position and strength of the other men on the defense?

A. If the fullbacks come out to meet the dribbler, set up the triangle-play pattern, or occasionally push a lead pass over the heads of the defense or try to dribble by. Try many ways of getting by a defense until you hit their weakness, then hit it to your advantage.

Q. When one fullback goes out to tackle a wing forward, does the other back up to cover and keep the center well guarded?

A. If the fullbacks do this, play in combination with the center forward or, more logically, try to cross to the other wing forward over the head of the deep fullback.

Q. Are their clearing kicks long, aimless kicks that are spectacular rather than accurate?

A. Set up to intercept.

Q. Do they switch with the wing halfbacks in covering the opponent's wing forwards and inside men?

A. If the fullbacks switch, be ready to set up own teammates while the opponents are making the switch and are a little disorganized.

Q. Does the goalie handle the ball well or does he fumble often and set up rebound plays for forwards driving in?

A. If the goalie is a poor ball-handler, the forwards should be driving to be right on top of the goalie to convert rebounds into scores.

Q. Is the goalie aggressive? Does he come out of his goal with good judgment?

A. If the goalie is aggressive, he will usually get the ball before the offense has a chance to play it for a shot at the goal. The strategy, obviously, is to keep the crosses out of the reach of the goalie. The forwards should be playing just on-side and driving in to pick up the crosses before the goalie has the chance. In fact, have one of your own men always in a position to pick up long kicks into the penalty box, and, especially, driving in hard for the kicks that the goalie has a chance to come out and play. Keep the pressure on the goalie by always driving in hard. Avoid long kicks that land way out of the reach of the forwards and are easy gets for a goalie driving out. Forwards should keep driving hard and make the goalie think twice before he comes out of the mouth of the goal.

Q. Does the goalie use good judgment in coming out to play crosses and solos?

A. Same as above.

Q. Does he handle a ground ball better than fly balls?

A. Play his weakness.

Q. Can he go to either side well or is he slower going to one side than the other?

A. Play his weakness.

Q. Does he position himself well in playing shots from the field?

A. If the goalie overplays, pass off and set up teammate on opposite side.

Q. Can he throw well and does he have a habit of throwing it to any one place or man more than another?

A. If the goalie has definite habits of always doing the same thing in the same situation, play them, and the percentages of intercepting and scoring will be in your favor. Consider stereotyped patterns as weaknesses on the goalie's part.

Q. If he kicks, does he kick it aimlessly or with a purpose in mind?

A. Diagnose first, then set up to intercept in both situations.

Q. Does he work well with his fullbacks or are they confused in covering and setting up for balance in the defense among them?

A. If the two fullbacks and goalie do not work well as a defensive unit, a few quick short passes in or around the penalty box might set up a wide open shot at the goal.

Q. What do you know about the field and the position of the sun during the time your game is to be played?

A. If the sun is high at the start of the game, play facing it the first period so that in the fourth period when the sun is low it will be behind you.

Q. Does the sun handicap the play of the goalie when the team takes one end of the field the first period any more than it would if the team picked the goal at the other end of the field?

A. Same as above.

Q. Does the sun affect the play of the goalie on a ball coming in from the side, coming in from the front, coming in low or coming in high?

A. Same as above.

Q. Does the field have a thick, soft, even grass top or is it scrub grass and bumpy or a skin top with bumps all over the field?

A. Smooth surface favors the short passing game; rough ground favors the long passing game.

Q. Will weather have to be taken into consideration the day of the game and will it have much to do with the type of game played?

A. If it is raining and wet, the ball will be harder to control; hence, the long passing game will be more effective. Hard kicks in front of the goalie are very hard to handle on wet days. With a strong wind behind your attack more liberties can be taken on the defense. The wind is your ally when it is behind you and should be used as such. Kicking into the face of the wind will call for a ground or short passing game and a deeper W formation attack.

VI

Diagrams—Game Situations

A TEAM offense and defense is merely the blend of many game situations which can be executed individually or in combination with other teammates. Certain game situations occur over and over again during the course of a game and when encountered should be handled with the minimum amount of effort and time. In short, the reaction to any game situation should be reflex and the percentages all in the player's favor of doing the right thing when faced with the situation during the game.

Obviously, knowledge of many or all game situations that are part of the game of soccer will help make a better player; however, knowledge, per se, is not the answer to successfully outwitting the opponent. Let me simply add that knowledge plus industry and constant repetition of each situation, which gives one the ability to act without thinking, will make the difference between successfully contending with or executing a game situation and unsuccessfully contending with one.

For all practical purposes each soccer player is a quarterback every time he gets the ball. When he gets the ball, he must decide quickly what is the best thing to do with the ball, and upon his

137

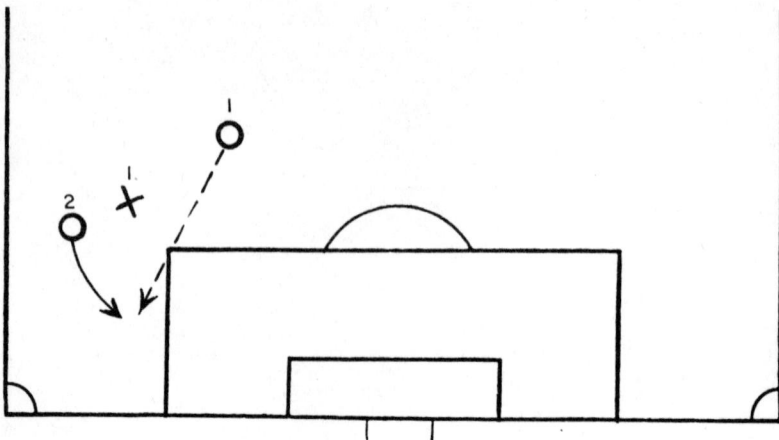

DIAGRAM 19   COMBINATION PATTERN BETWEEN THE
INSIDE AND THE WING FORWARD

A very much used and a very simple combination play is set up between the in-side and the wing forward. The inside passes to the wing forward cutting be-hind a back who is caught playing parallel to the wing forward. If the back plays out too far and gives the wing forward any opening at all to get behind him the offense should take immediate advantage of it. The pass can be a push pass on the ground from either the inside or the center forward. The same setup can be used between the wing halfback and the wing forward with a lob pass by the wing halfback over the head of defensive man X_1 for a lead pass to O_2 cutting behind X_1.

judgment, and his alone, depends his team's fortune at that par-ticular moment. Because of this, the more knowledge a player has of what to do in each situation, the better quarterback or player he will make. This means knowledge plus the ability to execute.

This chapter, then, is devoted to presenting many game situ-ations which should be studied and drilled with the idea of work-ing them into the team's offensive and defensive patterns.

COMBINATION PATTERNS

The use of combination patterns is based on the simple as-sumption that two or more men can do the job much easier and

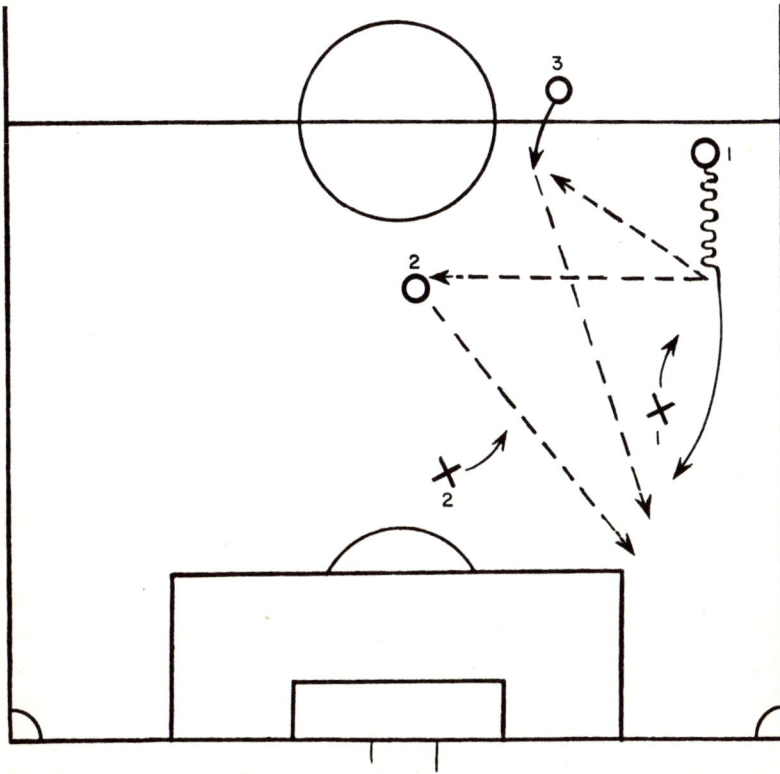

DIAGRAM 20   TWO-ON-THREE COMBINATION

A two-on-three combination will usually revert to a two-on-one situation or a clear field for one of the players with many fine opportunities. O1 dribbling down the side draws X1, the defensive back, and passes off to either O2 or O3. If either gets the pass he passes to O1 who, after he passes off cuts behind X1. If O3 is not covered he has the alternatives of dribbling and drawing, or crossing, or setting up a two-on-one situation with O2. In any event, a simple, cool, intelligent movement of the ball will give the offensive team the best scoring opportunity.

more successfully than one. With such patterns soccer is played as a team game on a sound, intelligent basis and results in a variety of attack.

All combination patterns should be set up with one or more of the following purposes in mind:

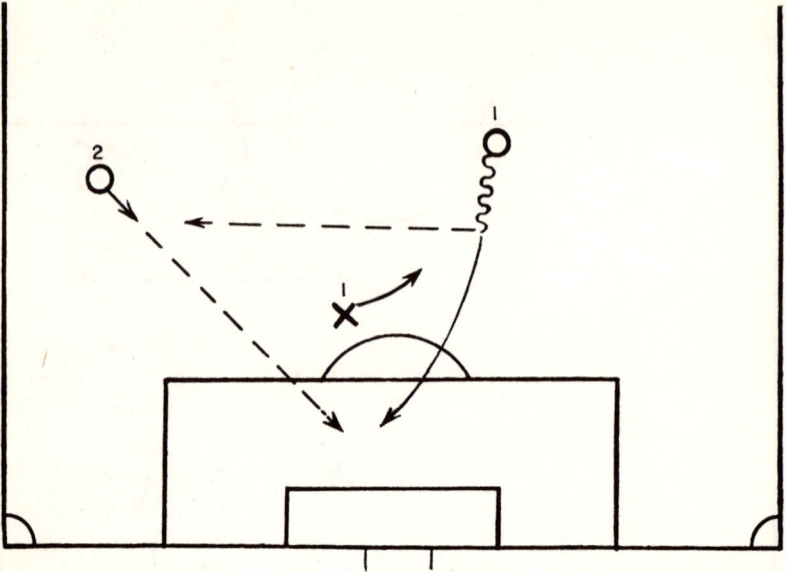

DIAGRAM 21   THE TRIANGLE PLAY

The simplest combination play is two offensive men working together to get the ball by one defensive man. The man with the ball dribbles and draws the one defensive man and passes off to his teammate. The passer immediately cuts behind the defense toward the goal, after the pass, setting himself for the repass. The passer should always be trying to get behind the defense for the return lead pass. $O1$ draws $X1$ and passes off to $O2$; $O1$ then cuts behind $X1$ for a return lead pass from $O2$.

1. To get behind the defense.
2. To advance the ball down the field.
3. To decoy a man out of position to open a spot or a lane to the goal for a teammate.

In setting up combination patterns keep the following basic principles in mind:

1. Two-on-one situation—the dribbler draws, passes off, drives behind the defense for a repass.
2. Three-on-two situation—the dribbler again draws, passes off to the open man and drives behind the defense for a repass.

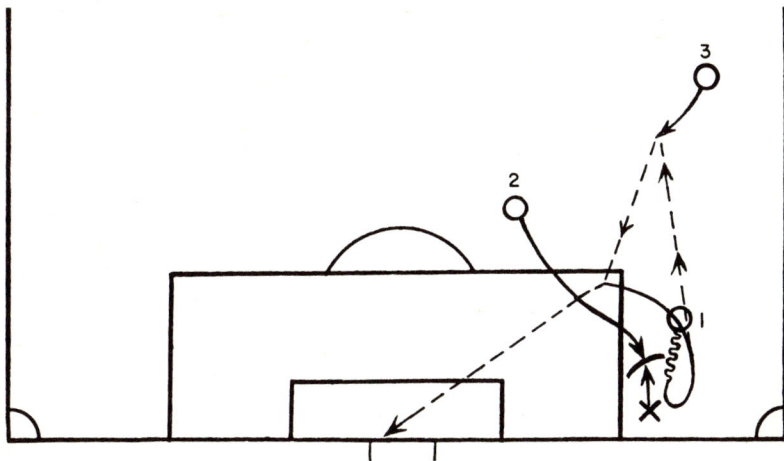

DIAGRAM 22   A SIMPLE COMBINATION PATTERN
INVOLVING WING FORWARD, INSIDE,
AND WING HALFBACK

Wing O1 dribbles down deep in corner, stops, pivots with body between defensive man and ball facing touch line, passes back to wing halfback O3. On pass inside O2 drives out behind and to the inside of wing O1 and O1's man X. Wing O1 drives around inside O2 to open spot left by inside forward O2 for a repass from halfback O3 and a shot at the goal. Inside O2 will in the process also set up a legal block on wing forward O1's man X. A variation of this can be O3 dribbling in for the shot or a pass over to an open halfback or a cross to the wing forward and inside driving in on the other side.

A three-on-two situation is played the same as the two-on-one.

3. Passes draws—passes off and immediately sets himself up for a repass.

DECOY PLAYS

A decoy play is a form of combination play used to draw a man out of position to open a lane toward the goal for a teammate. For a decoy play to be effective, the defensive man must be drawn away from his regular defensive position on the field. This will

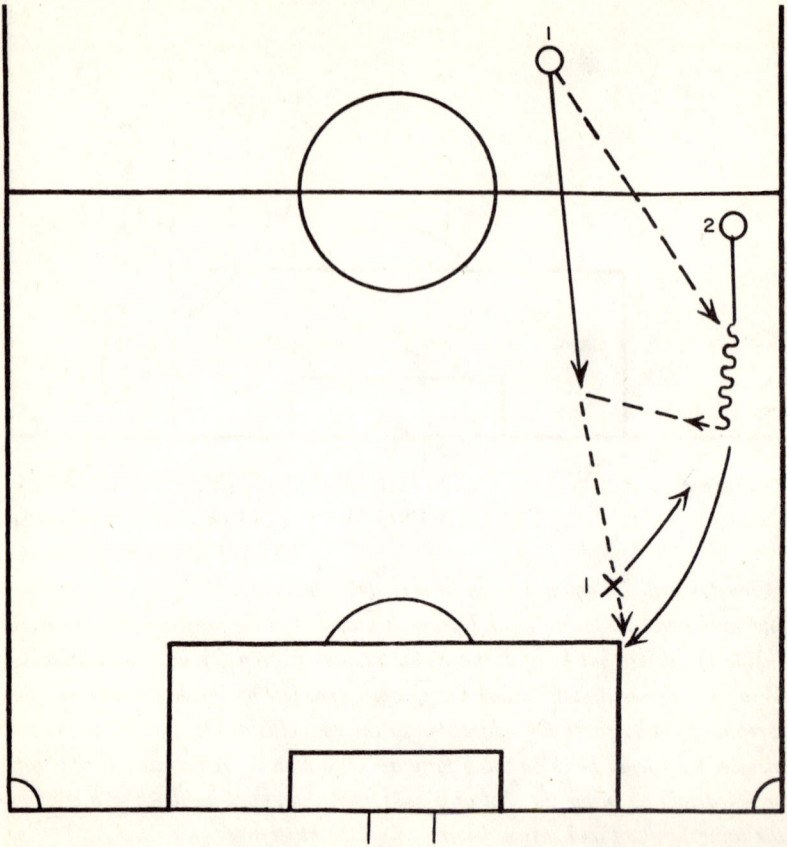

DIAGRAM 23   SIMPLE COMBINATION PLAY BETWEEN
THE WING FORWARD AND INSIDE IN
BRINGING THE BALL DOWN THE FIELD

Inside O1 passes ball down field to wing forward O2 who dribbles slightly to draw back X1. In the meantime inside O1 comes up field for repass from wing forward O2. On pass from O2 to O1 wing forward O2 immediately cuts behind back X1 for a repass and shot at the goal or pass to man coming down middle or other side of field.

open up the possibility of a teammate's moving into the open spot for a pass. If the defensive man does not go with the decoy, a pass to him will open up possibilities. A decoy move can also be used by an offensive man to open a spot on the field for himself. This

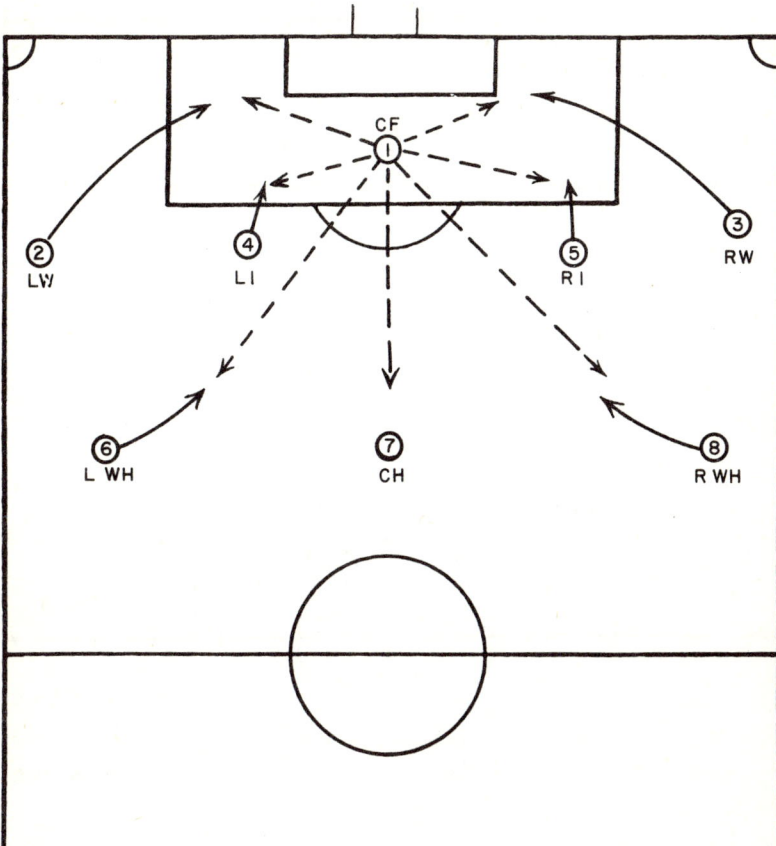

DIAGRAM 24   CENTER FORWARD PASSING POSSIBILITIES

The following diagram shows the center forward passing possibilities which should be creased in his mind. A good center forward will be an excellent passer who knows all his passing possibilities and is quick to take advantage of every one. He can pass off to either inside driving in for a shot. Pass off diagonally, on the ground between the defense, to one of the wing forwards who has cut behind the defense, or lob it over the heads of the defense for the wings to pick up, or pass back to the center halfback who might be open for a shot at the goal, or pass back to the wing halfbacks for a possible shot at the goal, or as a pass used to further open the defense with a subsequent pass to a man for a better shot at the goal.

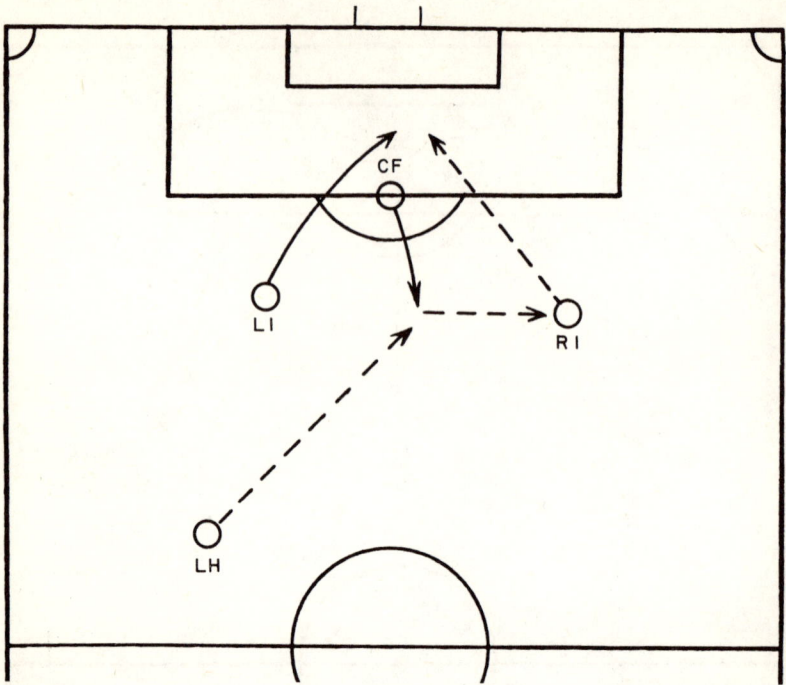

DIAGRAM 25   DECOY PLAY

Play to open up middle. Center forward comes out to meet pass on ground from left halfback which leaves the middle open. Center forward in turn passes to inside right. Inside left cuts to open spot that center forward cleared by his move and receives lead-spot pass from inside right.

is done by drawing his man out of position with the sole purpose in mind of opening up a spot and driving back in himself ahead of the defense for a spot-lead pass.

OPENING KICK-OFF LINE-UP AND PLAYS

The success of an opening kick-off play can have a great psychological effect on an opponent. Because of this, the opening kick-off should be considered more than the privilege of putting the ball into play. Plays can be worked out to meet every situation but to have them click—the choice of the play that best

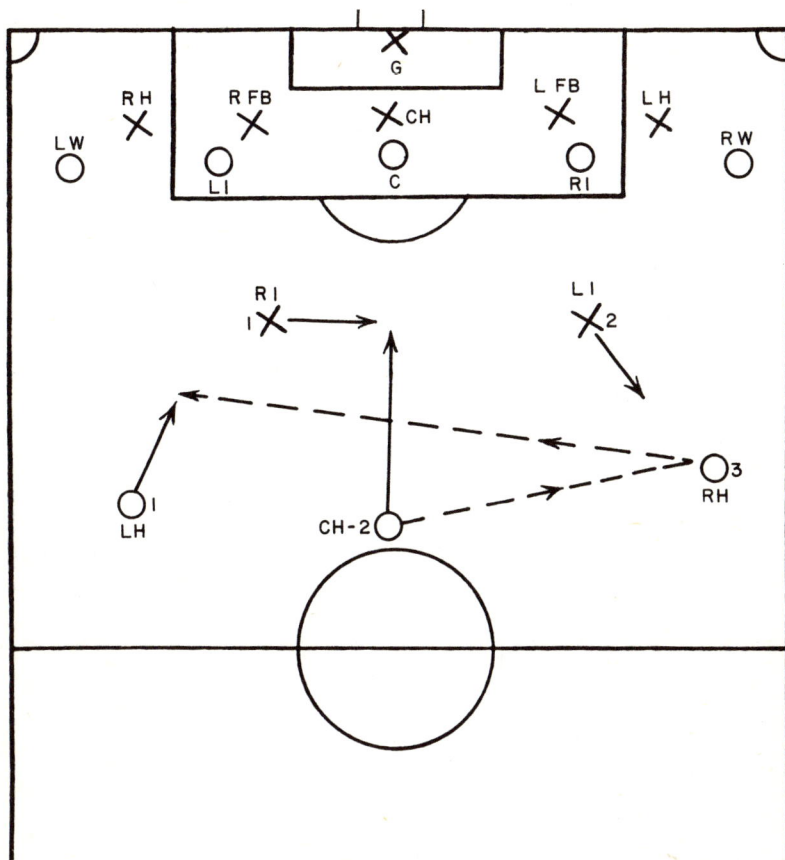

DIAGRAM 26   DECOY PASS AND MOVE BY THE CENTER
HALFBACK ON FREE KICK IN OFFENSIVE
END OF THE FIELD TO SET UP WING
HALFBACK FOR SHOT AT GOAL OR TO
OPEN UP DEFENSE FOR BETTER PASS
INTO THE FORWARDS

*Assuming that the two insides play the three halfbacks on defense, when O2
takes free kick and defensive insides play halfbacks loosely, O2 passes to O3.
This move pulls inside X2 out to pick up O3 and O2 then drives straight in
for goal. If inside X1 comes over to pick up O2, O3 passes over to other wing
halfback O1 who carries on as described above. O2's move of driving straight
in should be the decoy move to open up O1. All these passes must be on the
ground to make play click with little or no waste of time.*

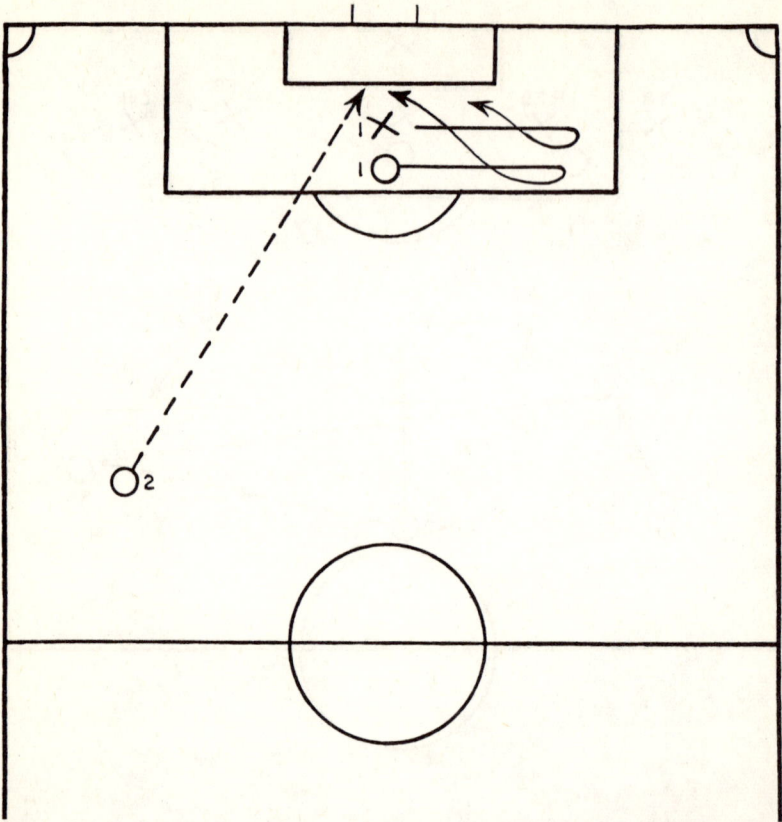

DIAGRAM 27   DECOY MOVE BY CENTER FORWARD
TO OPEN MIDDLE

*Center forward moves to side—if his defensive man goes with him he drives
back into the middle ahead of his man for a lead pass, best on the ground because it is easier to get control of. If the defensive man does not go with him
he can play out of position or switch position with a teammate and make his
openings from there. O1, center forward, moves out of the middle and draws his
man X1 out with him. He then immediately drives back into the middle ahead
of his man and a lead-spot pass from O2, his half. This move and subsequent
pass can be made by any two teammates. The object is to clear out a spot or
lane to the goal so a pass can be made to the open spot for the teammate clearing to drive in and pick up.*

fits the conditions at the time—repeated practice and alert, heads-up playing are requisites. For example, the choice of a play in which a cross kick is the key would certainly be a poor choice if that kick had to be made into the teeth of a strong wind. An opening kick-off play in which a long kick, with the wind, is the key kick, makes good sense and a possible quick score. On a windy day, plays should be used so that the key kick is with the wind, such as, a cross or a long kick down the field in front of the mouth of the goal.

GOAL KICK

Kicking Team.

1. Should have the advantage of knowing where the ball is going by the use of a simple set of signals.
2. The ball should be kicked to an open space usually, so that a wing forward, inside or center forward can pick up. As a rule if the defense is playing tight the kick should be to an open space with the offense set up so that they will be driving down the field to pick up the ball.
3. The team should note how the defense is set up to play the insides and wing forwards. Usually, kicking to a point between the middle of the field and side gives the advantage of two men, inside and wing forward, on one, the opposing wing halfback.
4. If the wing forward of the kicking team is successfully controlling the ball, he should send a cross to the opposite side of the field over the heads of the defense and too far out for the goalie to make a play on it.
5. The team should try to jockey their men out of position so that they are opening lanes and areas for the kicker.
6. The kicking team should know the strength of its kicker.
7. If the kick is with the wind, obviously all the positions, al-

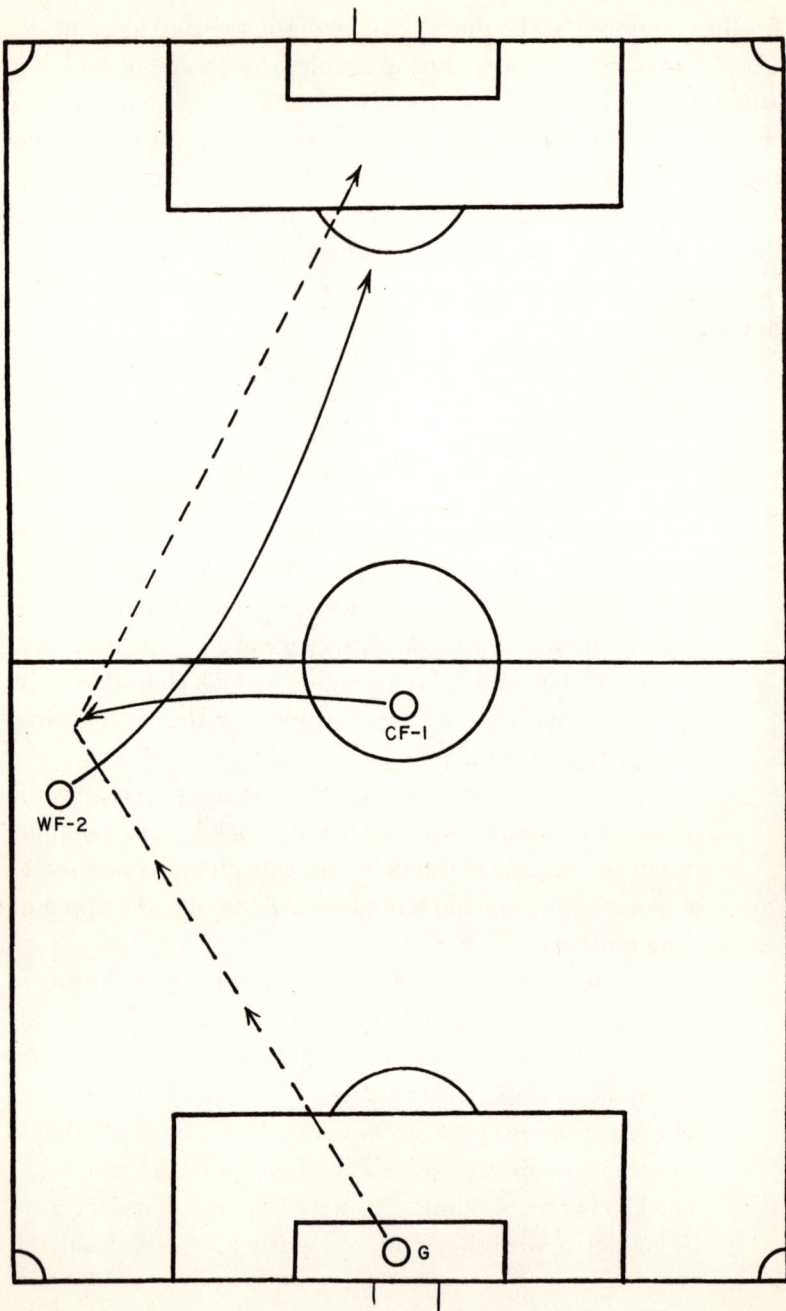

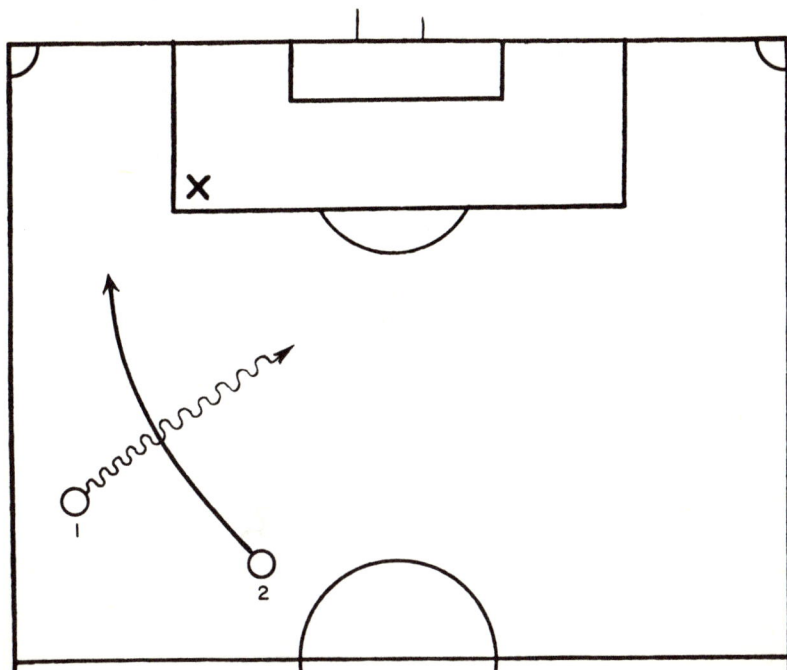

DIAGRAM 29   SWITCHING

One of the simplest switching maneuvers is between the wing forward and in-side O1. The wing dribbles into the middle and takes the ball down the lane ordinarily used by the inside. The inside, seeing this move, immediately swings out to cover and play the wing forward position left open by the wing forward. The reverse of this can be used with the inside dribbling the ball out and tak-ing it down the wing forward position with the wing forward switching into the inside slot.

DIAGRAM 28   DECOY MOVE INVOLVING CENTER
                           FORWARD AND WING FORWARD ON
                           THROW OR KICK FROM GOALIE

This play can be set up any time the goalie gets possession of the ball. Center forward O1 drives over to touch line and pulls his man with him. Goalie throws it to center forward by touch line. Wing on side of field to which center for-ward moves drives down to middle of field for spot-lead pass from center for-ward.

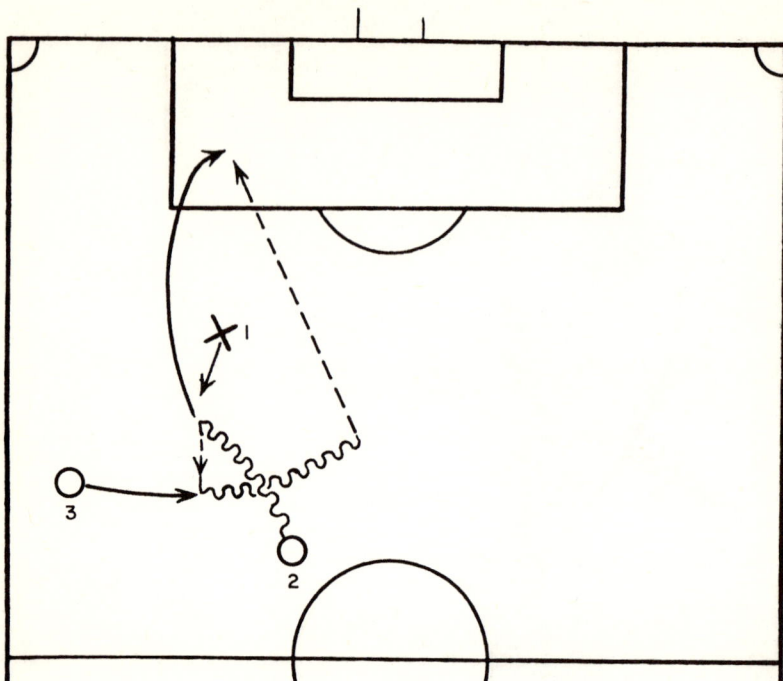

DIAGRAM 30   COMBINATION SWITCHING PATTERN
                  BETWEEN WING FORWARD AND INSIDE

O2, inside, dribbles toward touch line; on move O3, wing, cuts toward and behind O2; O2 passes off to O3 and takes one or two steps out toward touch line and then drives in diagonally to middle; O3 dribbles about two steps and drives a lead-spot pass for inside, O2, to pick up ahead of and behind the defense.

though still in the same relation to each other, will be farther down the field toward the opponent's goal.

8. The kick should be well placed and the kicker should be always studying the best possible place to put the ball so that his teammates can get control of it and make a subsequent fast break and a possible score.

9. If the kick is against the wind, the kicking team will have to play farther up the field, nearer the kicker.

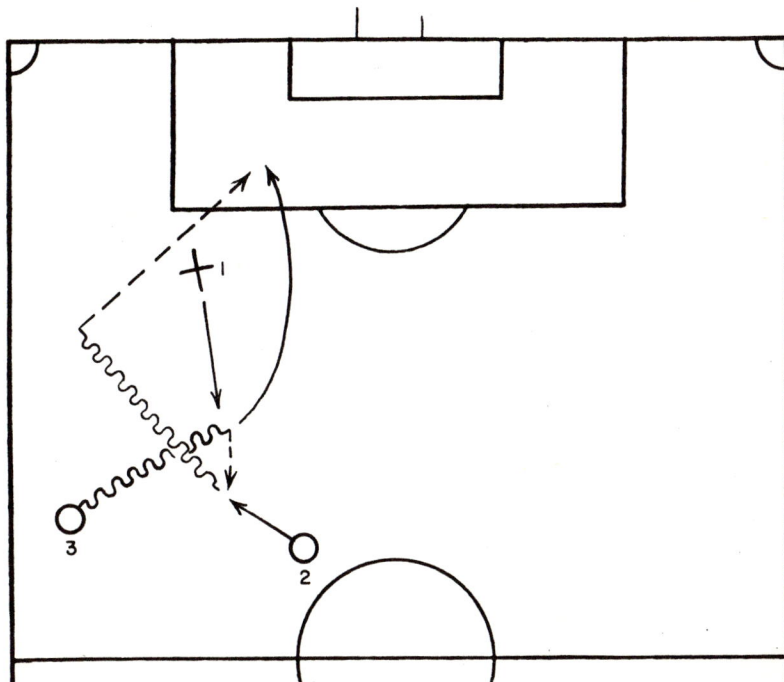

DIAGRAM 30A   COMBINATION SWITCHING PATTERN
                    BETWEEN WING FORWARD AND INSIDE

Reverse of Diagram 30 with wing forward O3 starting play.

10. The backs should definitely stay inside of the forwards to be ready to stop any immediate offensive thrusts.

Defensive Team (non-kicking team)

1. Each man should position himself so that he will be driving into the ball when making a play on it.
2. The play is usually a header and should be a pass to an open teammate. Each man should know the relative positions of his teammates and pass to one of them or to an open space so one of them can get it. Driving into the ball when heading it usually gives the man a better chance of getting

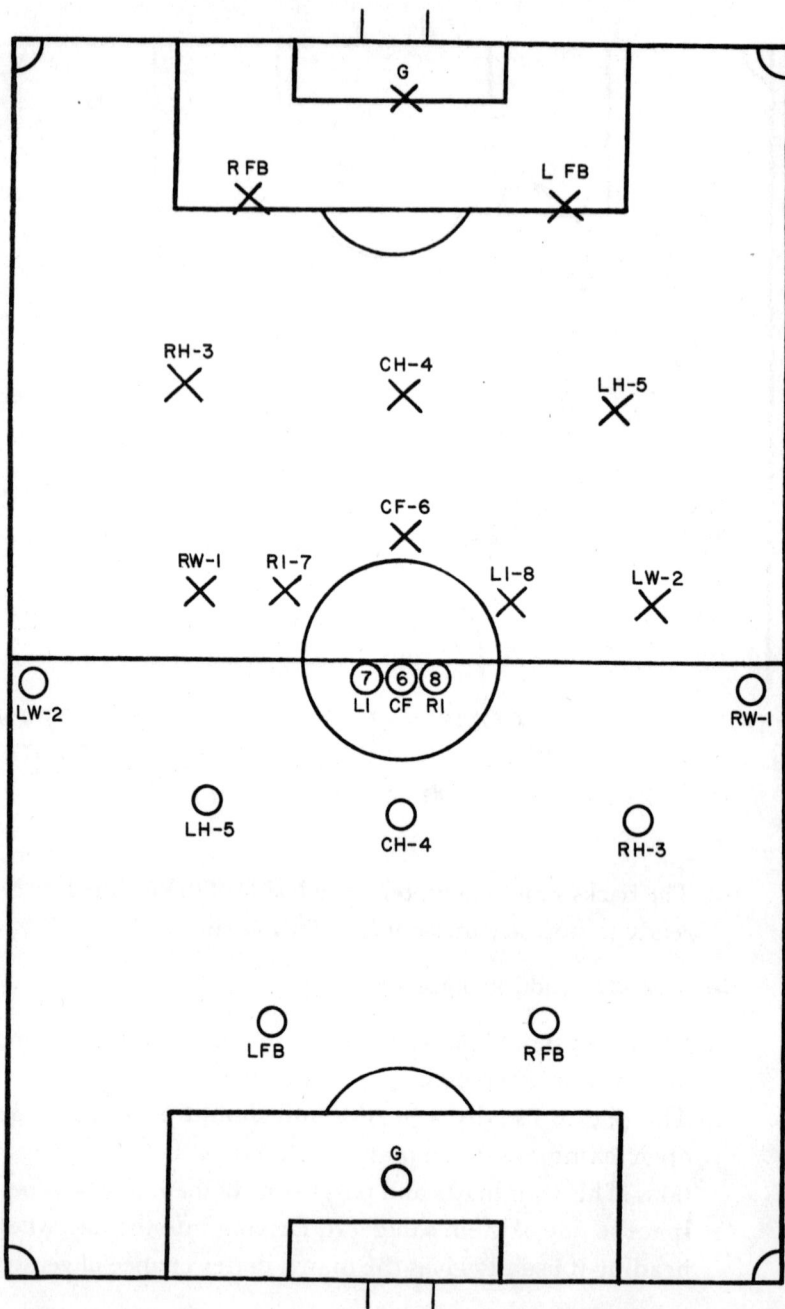

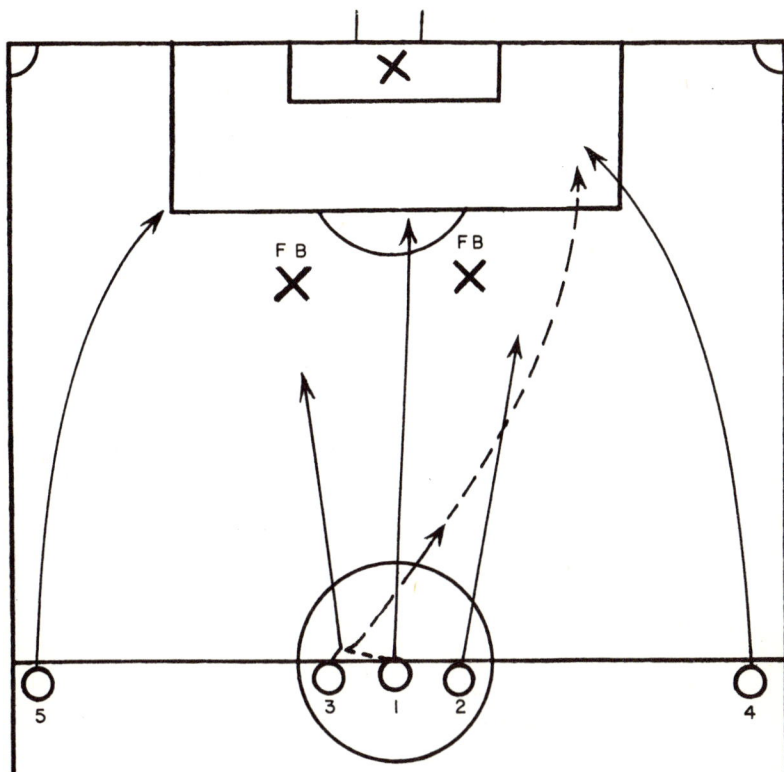

DIAGRAM 32   OPENING KICK-OFF PLAY

*In all opening kick-off plays the forwards who are not in the actual play should
be driving down to get in position to take immediate advantage of any break
that comes their way. This play is used if the fullbacks are playing up too close
together. This should be a two-pass play using the wind to advantage, if there
is one. O1 passes to O3 who in turn passes ball to wing O4 over and behind
the defense. The play can be to either side.*

DIAGRAM 31   OPENING KICK-OFF LINE-UP

Defensive assignments on kick-off: X1 checks O5

X2 checks O3	*X4 checks O6*
X3 checks O2	*X5 checks O1*

X6 drives in and picks up O4 if ball is passed back to him.

*X7 and X8 should hesitate a minute before driving in so as not to set up a
situation where the insides can dribble by them.*

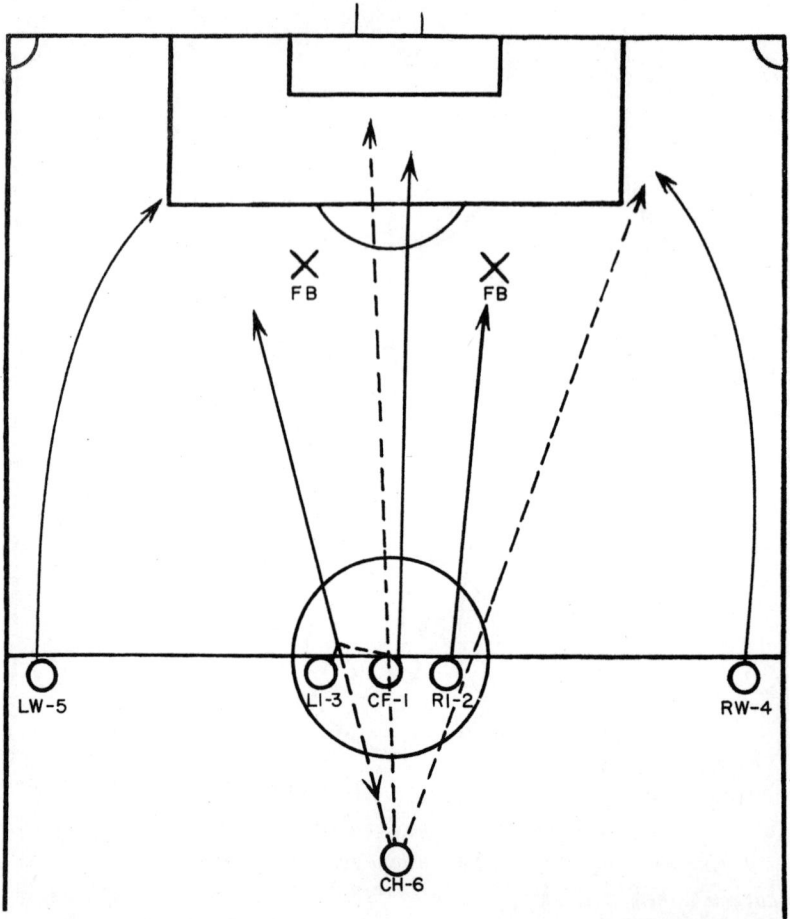

DIAGRAM 33   **KICK-OFF PLAY**

This play is used when the fullbacks are playing up the field and there is a good chance of the long kick being dropped over their heads behind them. The pass is from O2 or O3 back to the center half O6 who then makes the kick to the wing forward. If the fullbacks are playing way up, a kick, with the center halfback kicking, over the heads of the defense in the middle is very effective. All the forwards must be driving down on these plays.

it. If a halfback plays it, he should pass diagonally down the field for the wing forward or inside to pick up or down the middle for the center forward.

3. The team members should play the wind to their advantage.

4. The defensive team should remember that the kicking team has the advantage and not let the latter jockey them out of position.

5. The most logical place for the goal kick is diagonally down the field to a spot for the wing forward to pick it up. The defensive team should be ready for it.

6. The deep fullback should be ready for a cross in the event that the wing forward or inside or, for that matter, the center gets the ball.

7. Defense should organize as quickly as possible in the event that the kicking team gets control of the ball.

TOUCH LINE KICKS

On offense, touch line kicks in the defensive end of the field should be kicked down the same side of the field on which the kick is being taken. Any touch line kick across the field should be discouraged when taken deep in the defensive end of the field. The rule of thumb is that the farther away from your own goal line the kick is being taken, the more places there are to which the ball may be kicked. Touch line kicks, like all other free kicks, should not be kicked aimlessly and without purpose. The ball should be kicked to a definite spot so that the kicking team will gain first possession of the ball and then distance. The men on the kicking team should try to jockey their men out of position so that when the kick is taken they will be driving to the spot where the ball is to be kicked, and, hence, have the advantage in gaining possession of it.

There are conditions in which the kicker might be forced to pass

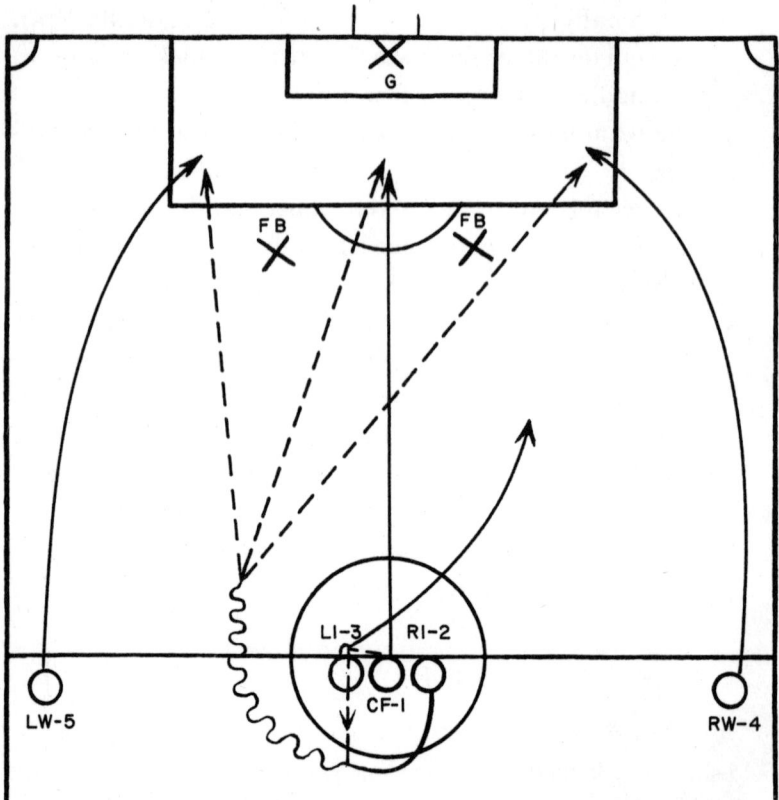

DIAGRAM 34   OPENING KICK-OFF PLAY

This play should be used against teams with opposing inside forwards driving in bull-like. This play is used when the three opposing inside forwards are driving in bull-like to block any forward passing. O1 passes to O3, who turns with his body well over the ball and passes back to inside O2 who has cut behind O1 and O3. O2 can then take a couple of dribbles and pass it to a spot around either corner of the penalty box for the wings O4 and O5 to drive in and pick up, or lob the ball over the defense to a spot just inside the front line of the penalty box for the center forward O1 to pick up on the drive and shoot. Inside O3 on play switches sides with other inside O2. The option on this play with men driving in is for inside O3 to side-step their onrush and start down the field himself, or for O2 to continue dribbling down the field until he draws a man.

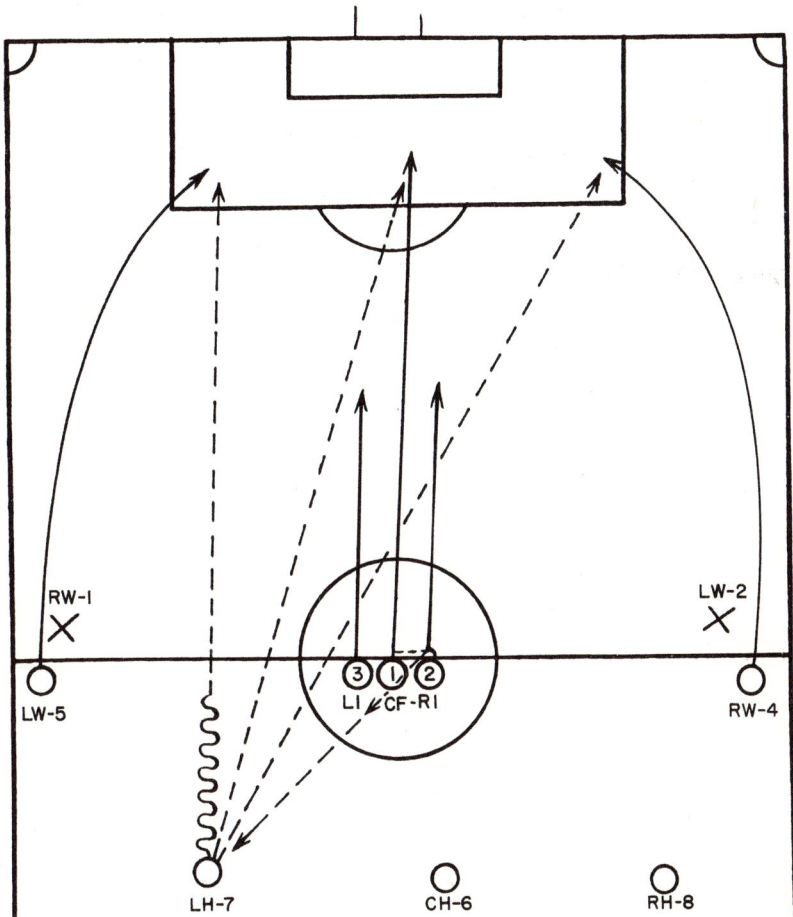

DIAGRAM 35   OPENING KICK-OFF PLAY TAKING
ADVANTAGE OF OPEN WING HALFBACK

*This setup is used when the wing forwards X1 and X2 on the opposite team
play near the touch line. With the opposing insides driving in to the middle
and wings playing the touch line it leaves things wide open for the wing halfbacks to dribble down and draw, pass down to wing on same side of field, cross
to wing on other side of field behind defense or down the middle to center forward. The halfback might have the chance of dribbling right in for a good shot
and if the opportunity presents itself he should not hesitate to do so.*

the ball off to a halfback or a man closer to him, such as, when the kick has to be made into a driving wind or in wet weather. When adverse conditions do exist, obviously, the kicker must weigh all factors and then use good judgment in putting the ball into play.

Defense on touch line kicks is the same as on free kicks. However, the deeper in the offensive and defensive territory the kick is taken, the more the players set up as they would for a corner kick.

DIAGRAM 36   POSSIBLE SUBSEQUENT PLAY WHEN
THE CENTER FORWARD PICKS UP CLEARING
KICK AND DEFENSIVE FULLBACKS ARE
PLAYING IN TANDEM

Fullback O1 clears the ball to center forward O3 who immediately kicks a lead pass over fullback's (X1) head for wing forward O2 to drive down the field and pick up. If O2 can go all the way for the shot he should. On the other hand, if fullback X2 comes over to cover, O2 should cross a pass ahead to the other wing forward O4 who can pick it up and drive in for the shot.

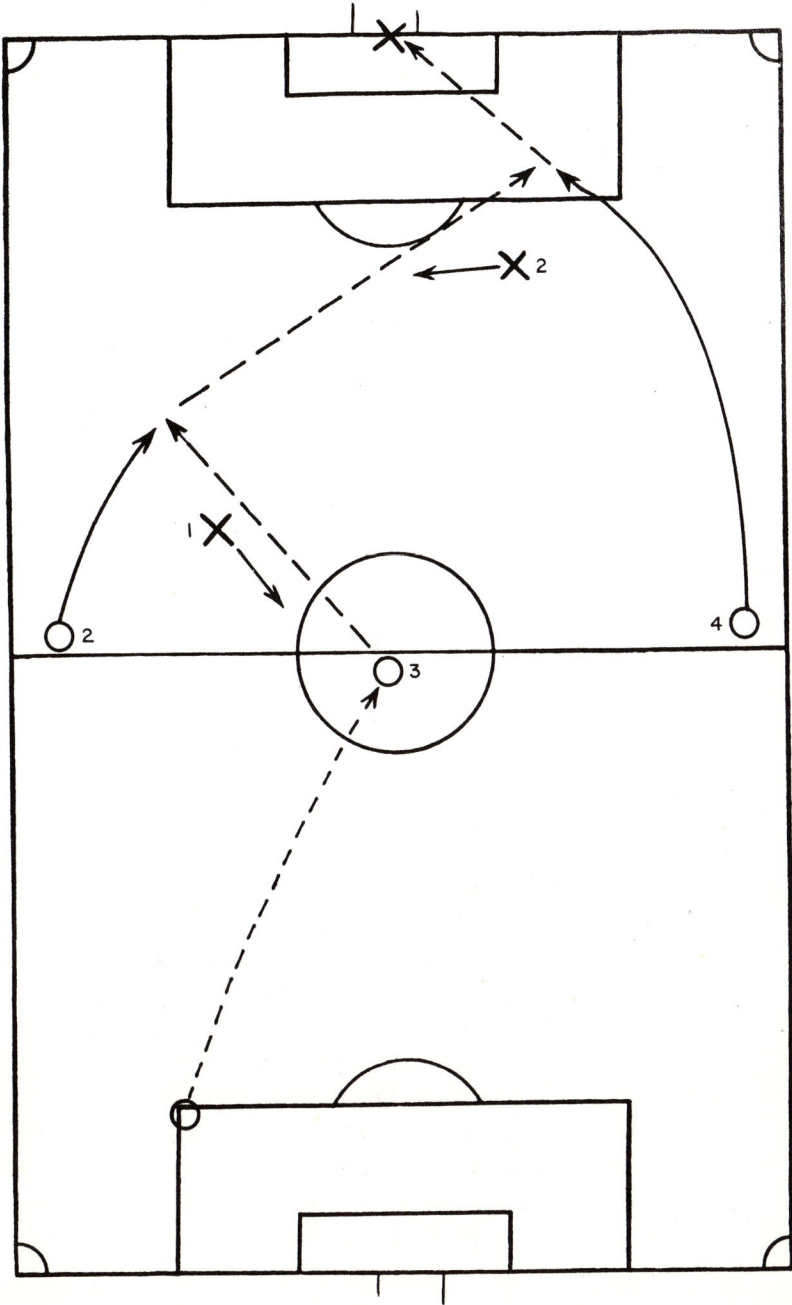

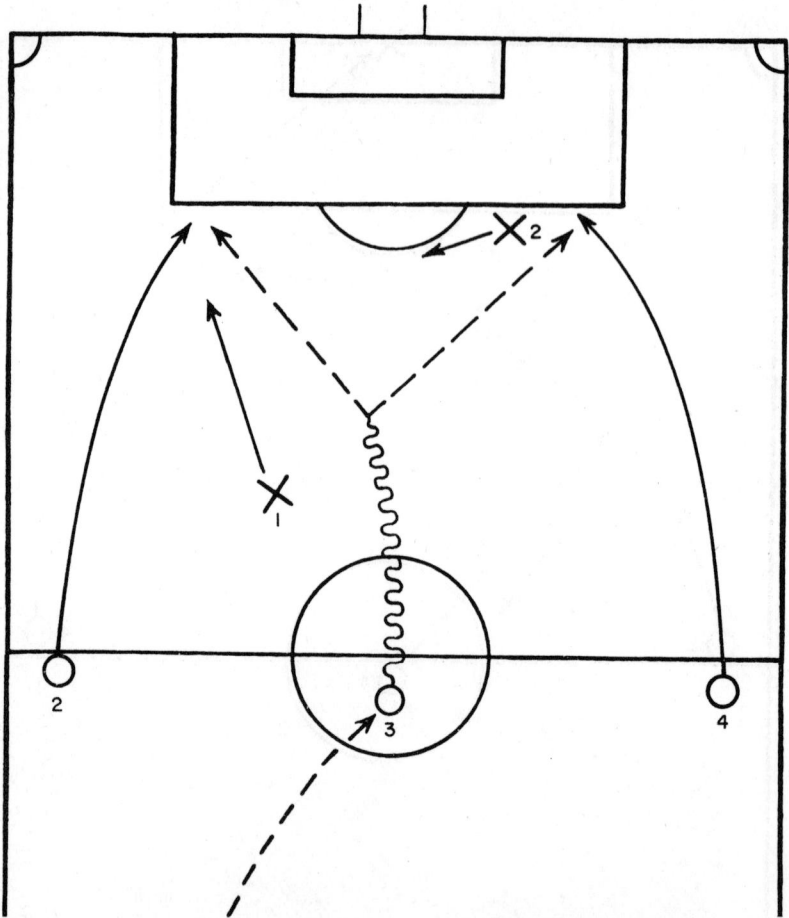

POSSIBLE SUBSEQUENT PLAY WHEN
CENTER FORWARD PICKS UP CLEARING
KICK AND DEFENSIVE FULLBACKS ARE
PLAYING TANDEM AND DROP BACK

Center forward O3 picks up clearing kick from fullback (not shown). O3 sizes up the situation; when upfield fullback X1 drops back O3 dribbles down the center. If fullback X2 comes over to cover the middle, center forward O3 immediately pushes a lead pass to wing O4 who drives in for the shot. If X1 comes over to cover center forward, O3 can push a lead pass behind fullback X1 for wing forward O2 to pick up and drive in for the shot.

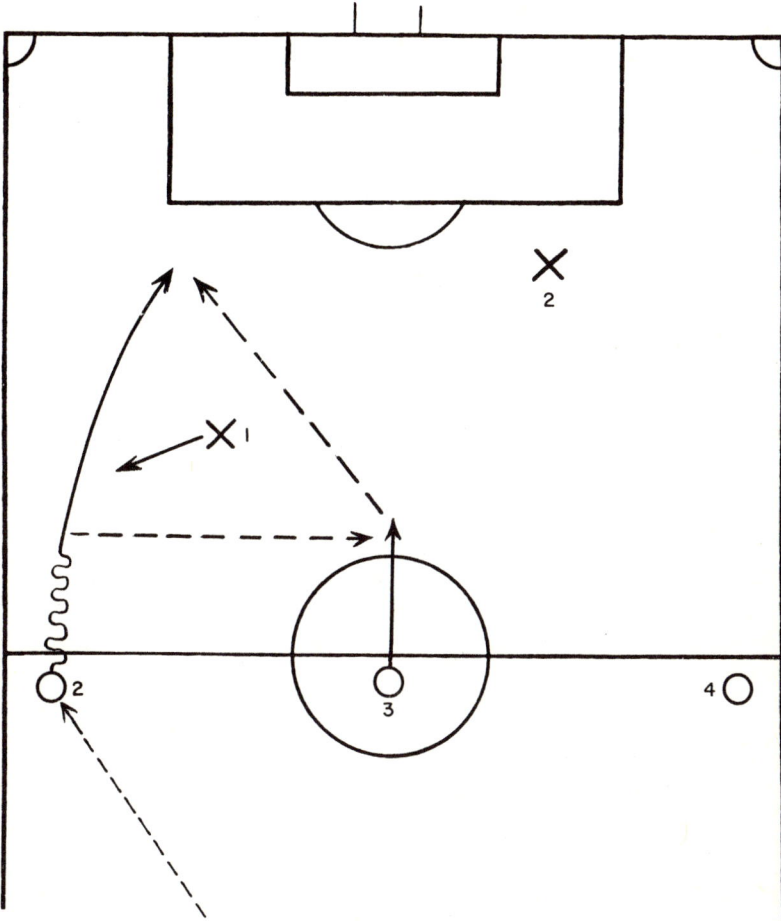

DIAGRAM 38   POSSIBLE SUBSEQUENT PLAY WHEN
WINGS PICK UP CLEARING KICK AND
DEFENSIVE FULLBACKS ARE IN TANDEM

*After wing forward O2 picks up clearing kick from fullback O1 he can pair
up with the center forward O3 and work the triangle on X1. That is, O2 dribbles
and draws X1 and pushes a pass to O3 who immediately pushes a lead pass
behind fullback X1 for O2 to pick up and drive in for the shot. The other possibility is for O2 to immediately cross ball over and down the field to wing forward O4 to pick up. However, the first move seems to be the more effective against
the tandem fullback setup, unless the cross can get behind the deep fullback.*

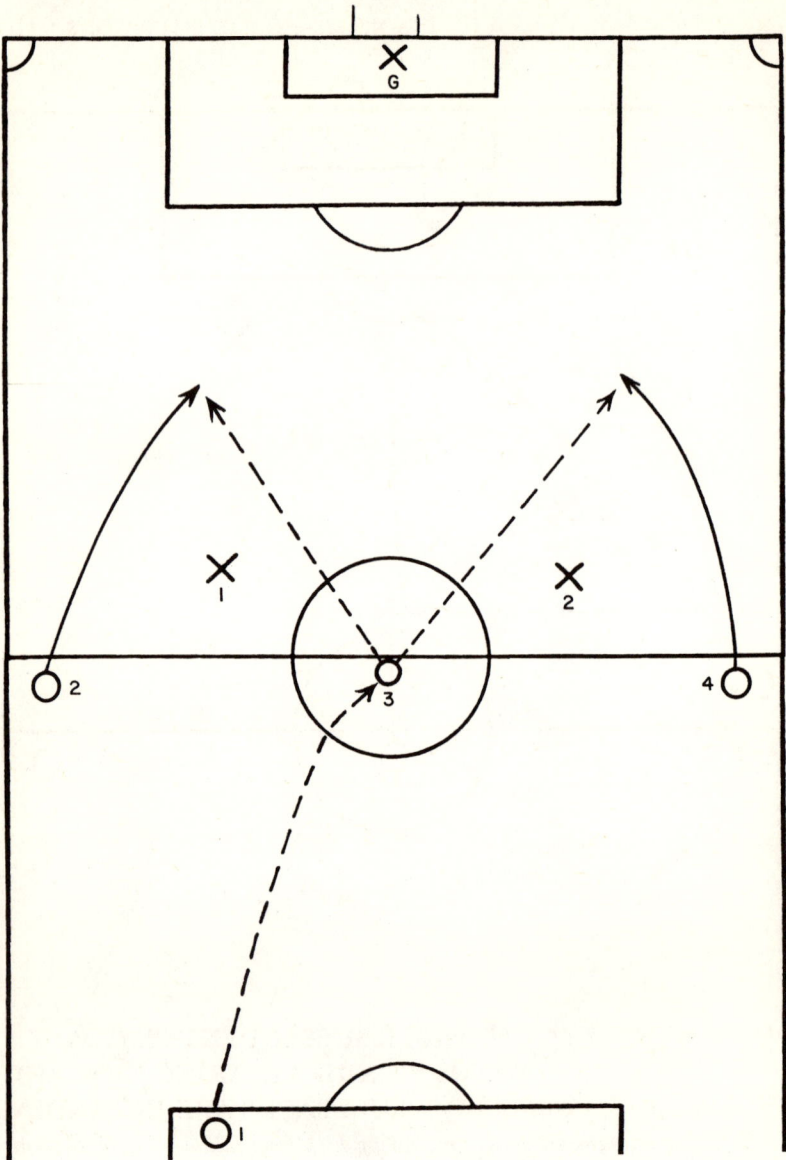

DIAGRAM 39   MOST EFFECTIVE SUBSEQUENT PLAY FOR
CENTER FORWARD WHEN HE PICKS UP A
CLEARING KICK AND DEFENSIVE
FULLBACKS ARE PLAYING PARALLEL

Fullback O1 clears to center forward O3 who immediately kicks down to either
side of the field out of the reach of the goalie for either wing forward to drive
in, pick up ball and shoot.

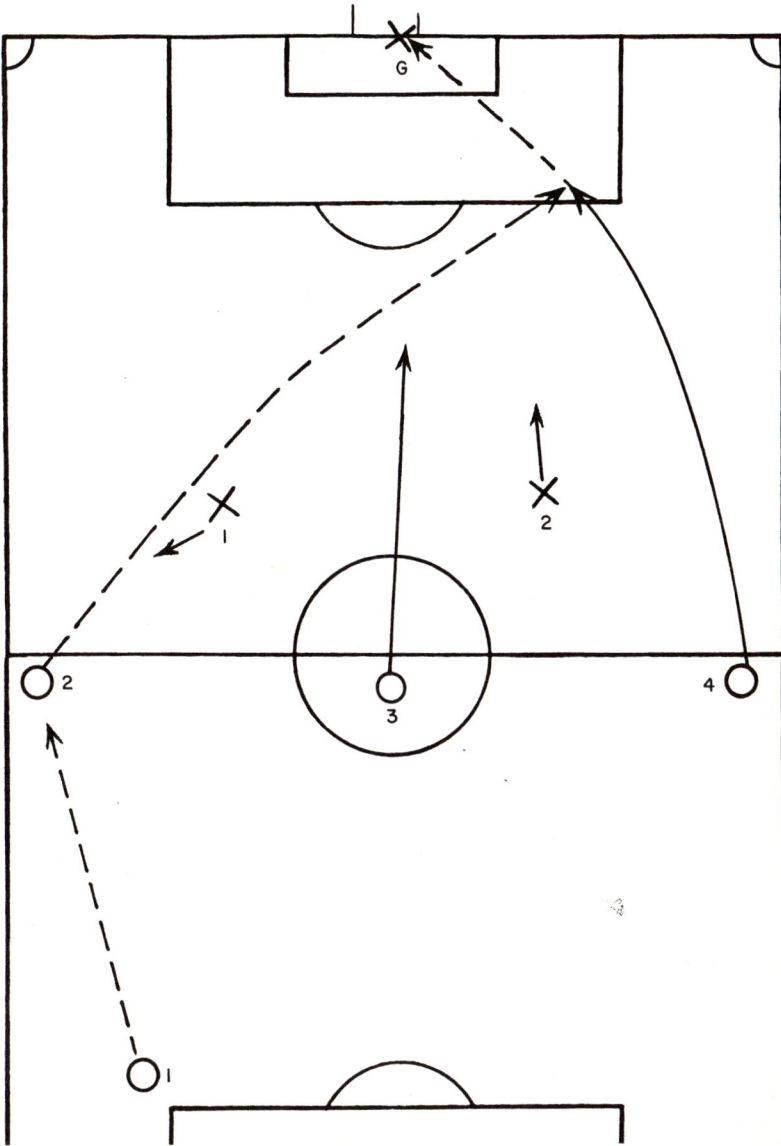

DIAGRAM 40   MOST EFFECTIVE SUBSEQUENT PLAY
WHEN WING FORWARD PICKS UP A
CLEARING KICK WHEN FACED WITH
DEFENSIVE FULLBACKS PLAYING UP THE
FIELD ON PARALLEL LINE

*O1 clears to O2 who immediately crosses ball over and down the field and be-
hind the defense for winger O4 to pick up and drive in for shot.*

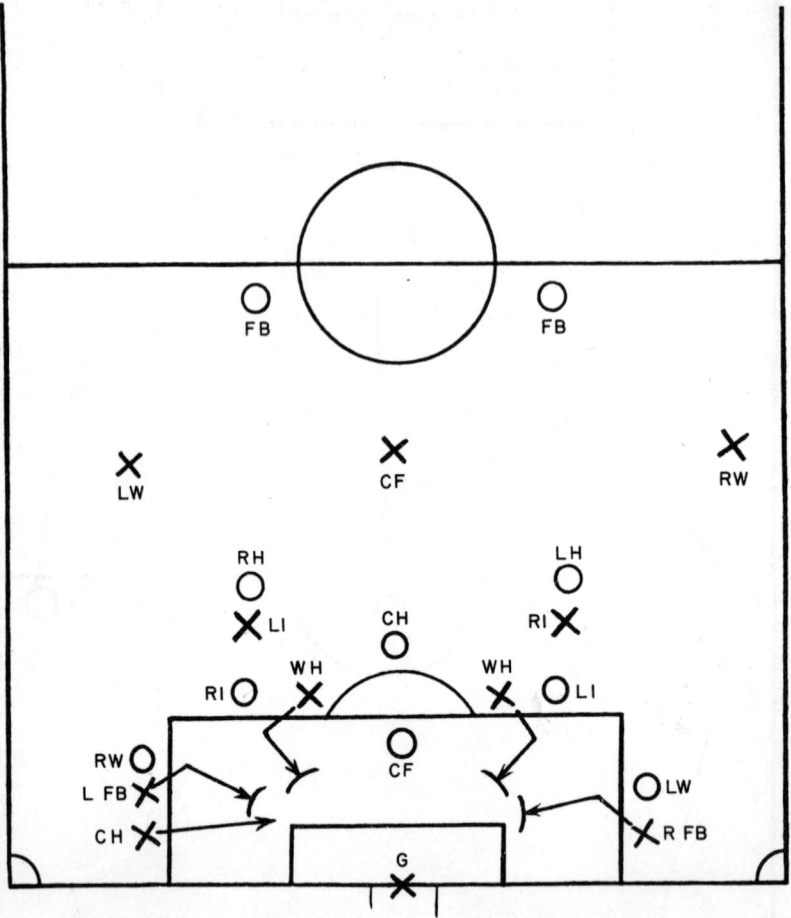

DIAGRAM 41   PENALTY KICK LINE-UP—OFFENSE
                                              AND DEFENSE

Center forward taking kick—when the center forward takes the kick the center halfback positions himself as in diagram—to get edge in the event of a rebound. In this diagram the defensive men are all playing inside of their men exactly as they should, so that, in the event of a rebound they can obstruct and slow down the forward progress of their men and drive in for the ball ahead of their man and between their man and the ball. For the men on the offense to get the edge they should try to position themselves between their men and the goal.

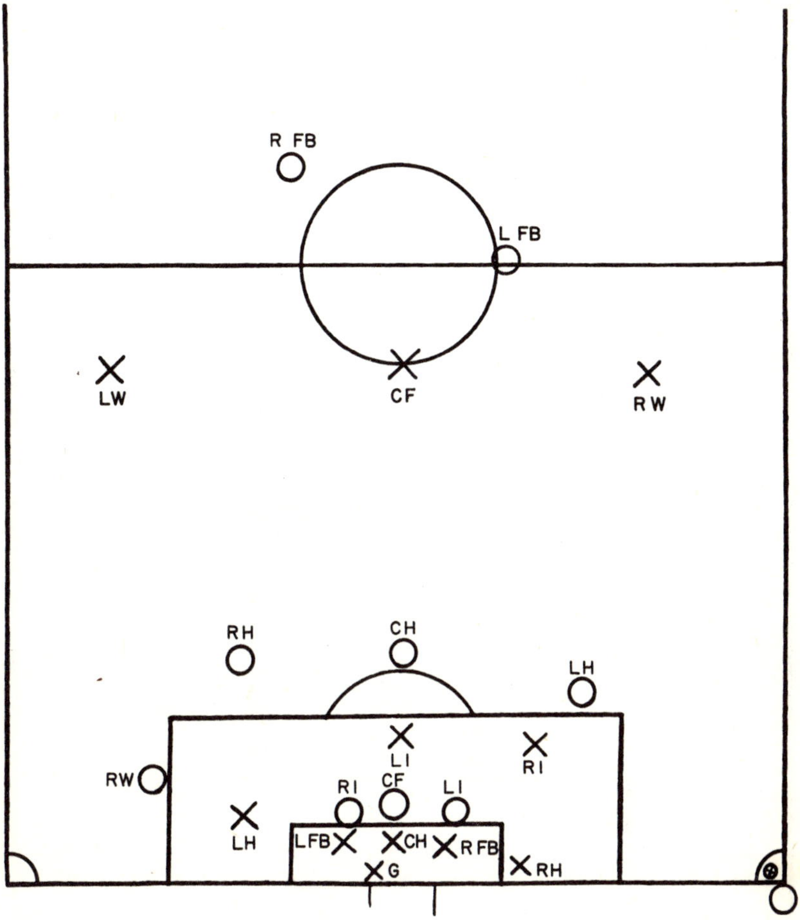

DIAGRAM 42   CORNER KICK LINE-UP—OFFENSE
                                                AND DEFENSE

Line-up for both offensive and defensive men on corner kicks. The defensive men should stay between their men and the opponent's goal and always try to keep their eyes on the ball and the man they are guarding.

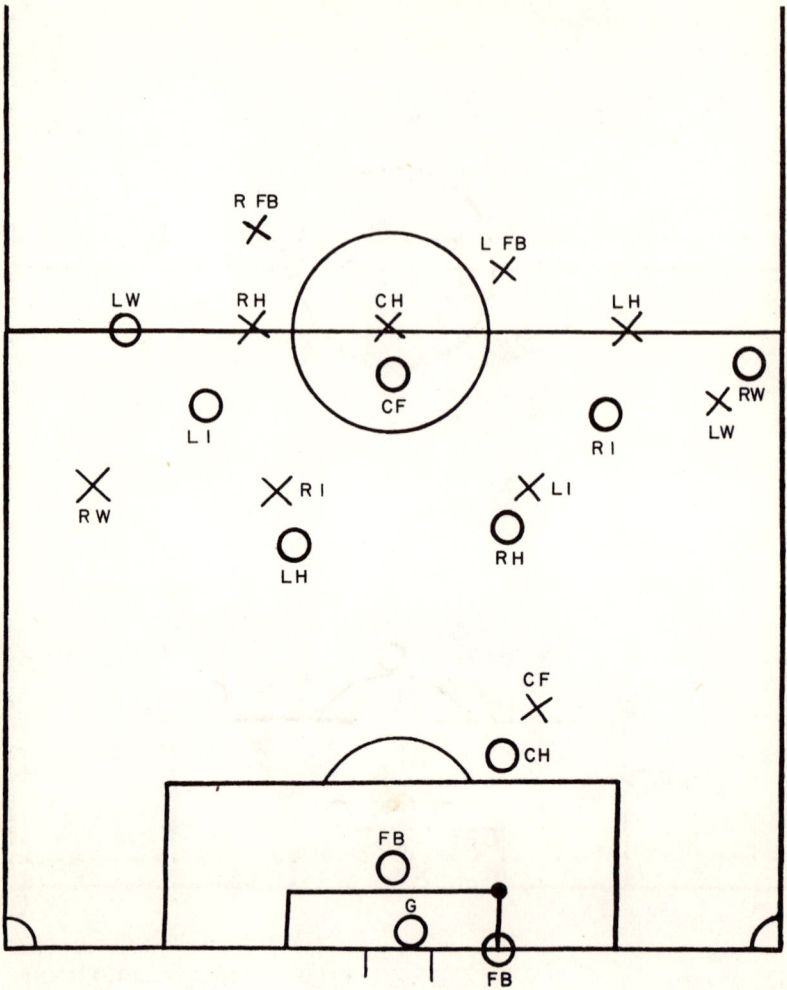

DIAGRAM 43   GOAL KICK LINE-UP—OFFENSE
                                          AND DEFENSE

The fullbacks in this setup must be ready to pick up the wing forwards. Some coaches on defense prefer having the insides pick up the insides and wing halfbacks play the wing forwards. Unless unusual circumstances exist, such as wet weather or kicking into a strong wind I prefer having the insides on the kicking team down the field in an offensive position ready to make the goal kick a definite offensive thrust.

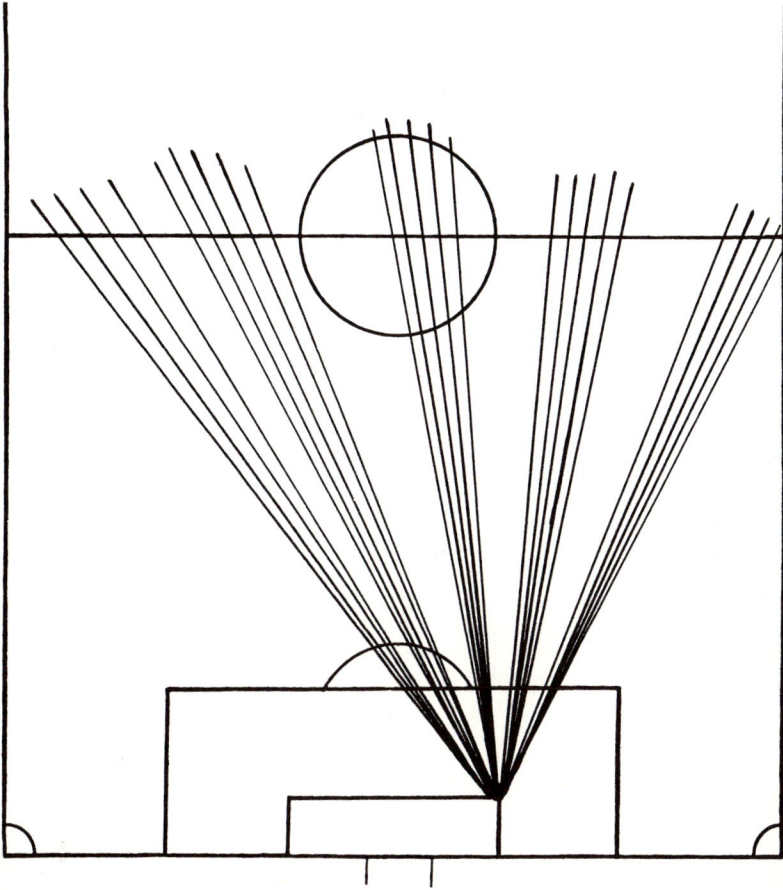

DIAGRAM 44   GOAL KICK—POSSIBLE PASSING LANES
FROM GOAL KICK

The goal kicker has the possible passing lanes as shown above in which to kick the ball down the field to one of his men or to an open spot. He can kick down one of the shaded lanes which will be to a man or down the lanes that are not shaded which will be to a spot. Since there are many goal kicks during the game everything possible should be done to get control of the ball when the kick is taken. Signals should be used so that every man on the team will know where the ball is going. Lanes or spots can be numbered. The important thing is that every man on the kicking team knows where the ball is supposed to be kicked so that they can get the jump on the opponents.

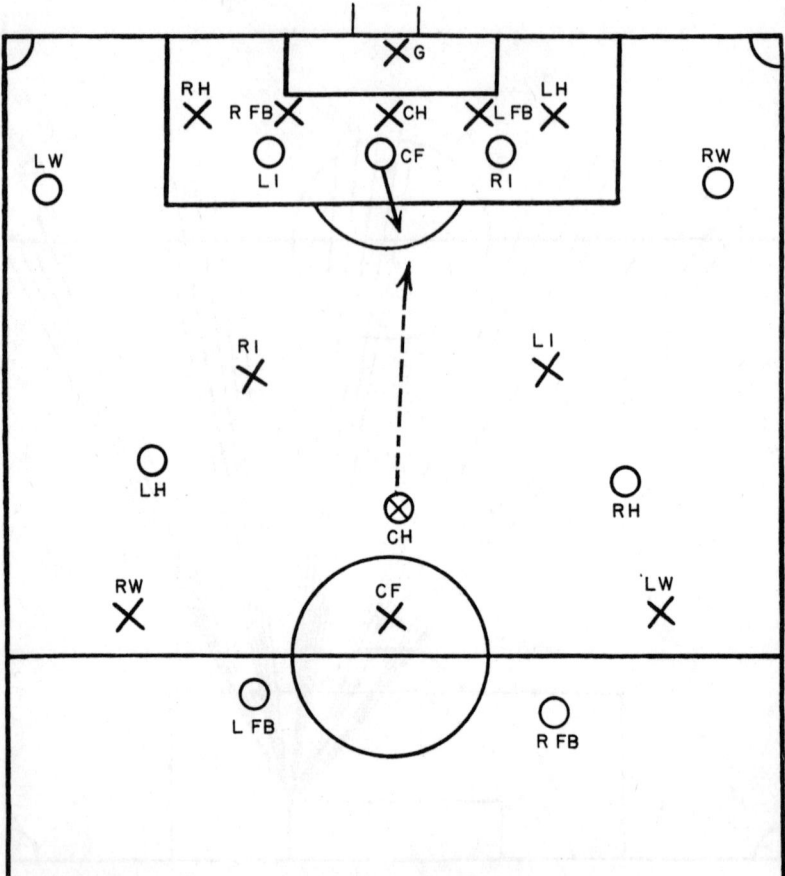

DIAGRAM 45   DIRECT FREE KICK LINE-UP—
                              DEFENSE PLAYING TOO FAR BACK

In this diagram the line of defense is too far back, since a kick could place the ball in front of the line of defense where the offensive team could drive out to pick it up. With the free kick dropped in front of the defensive line for the center forward to pick up, it opens many play possibilities which a good center forward will take immediate advantage of.

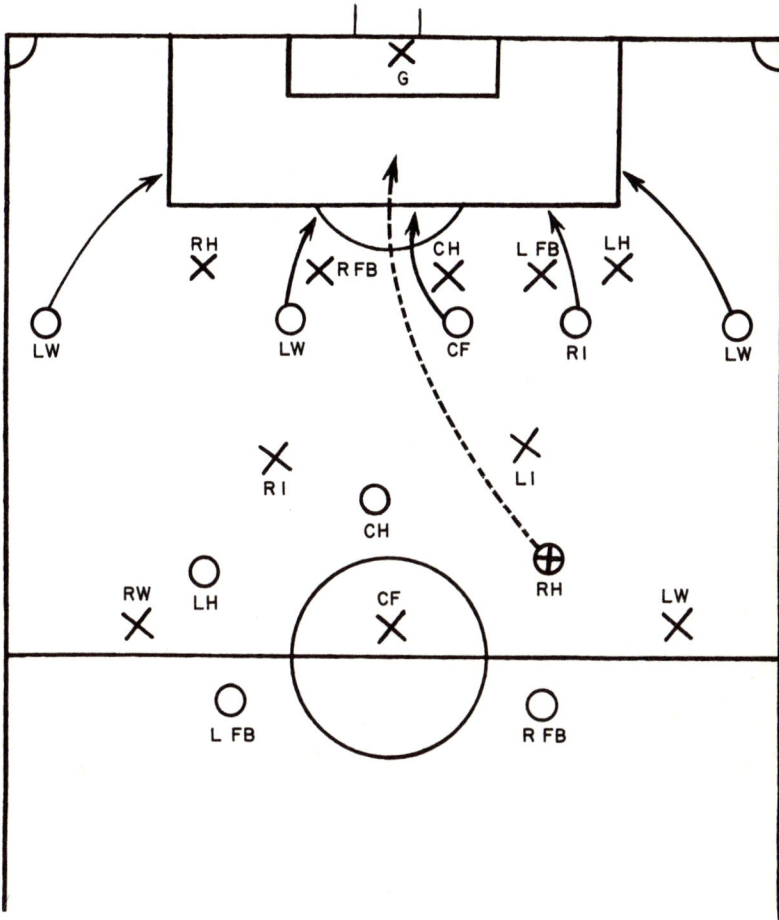

DIAGRAM 46   DIRECT FREE KICK SITUATION—
LINE OF DEFENSE TOO FAR OUT

Line of defense too far out, since ball can be dropped over the heads of the defensive men on the line with no chance of the goalie getting the ball before the onrushing forwards driving in. Goalie must have his eye on the ball all the way in all free kick situations.

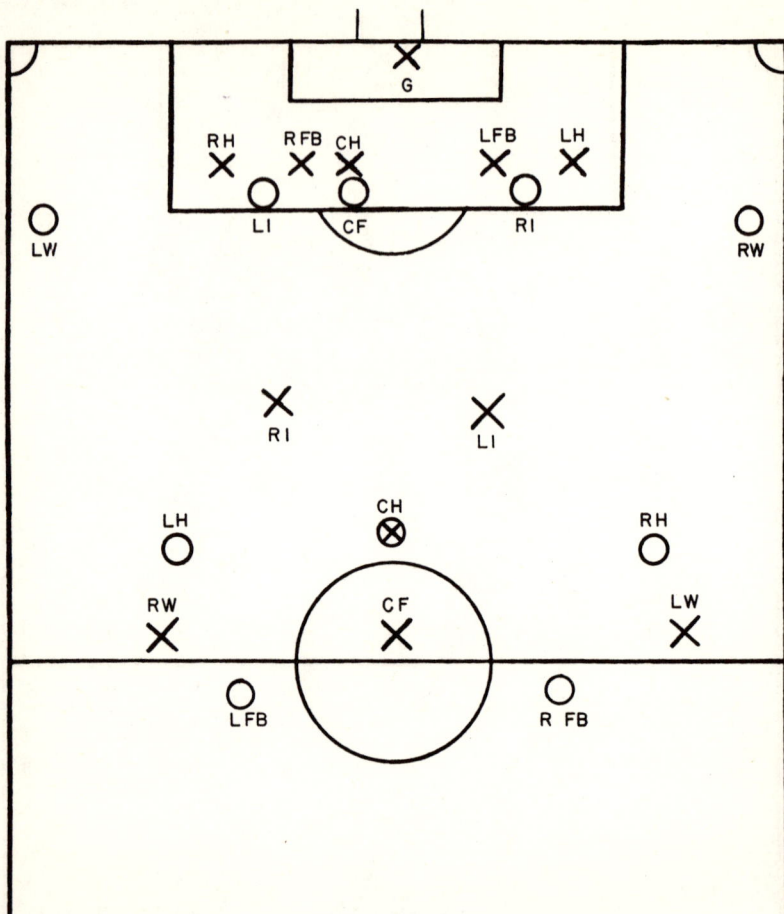

DIAGRAM 47   DEFENSIVE LINE PROPERLY PLACED

Defensive line properly placed since it gives the goalie a chance to play the ball before the opponents, in the event the ball is lobbed over the defensive line. If the ball is kicked before the defensive line there is no damage done and a good chance for a play on the ball by a defensive man driving out.

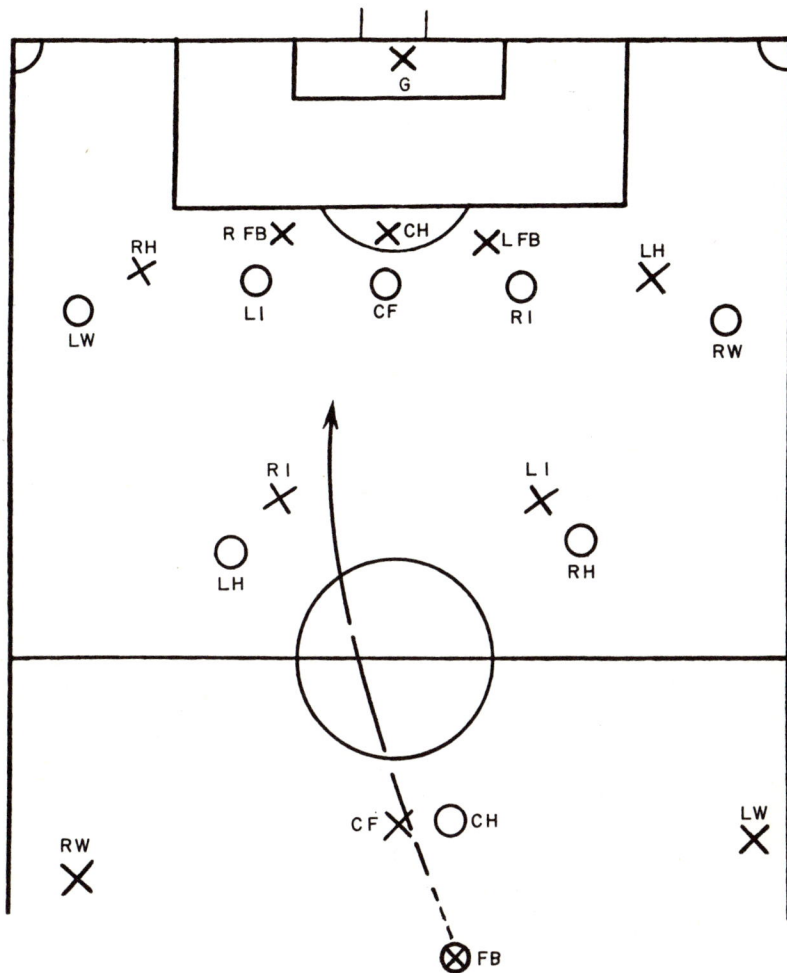

DIAGRAM 48   DIRECT FREE KICK SITUATION—
FREE KICK TAKEN FROM THE DEFENSIVE
END OF THE FIELD

When a free kick is taken deep from the other end of the field the defensive line is properly placed when no kick can possibly be kicked over their heads and they are in a good position to drive forward into the ball for a play. The defense must be alert to check every possibility for a cross or any other offensive development that the kicking team might try to set up. As soon as the fullbacks and halfbacks realize they cannot make a play on the ball, or their man is not going to make a play on the ball, they should drop back and be ready to cover.

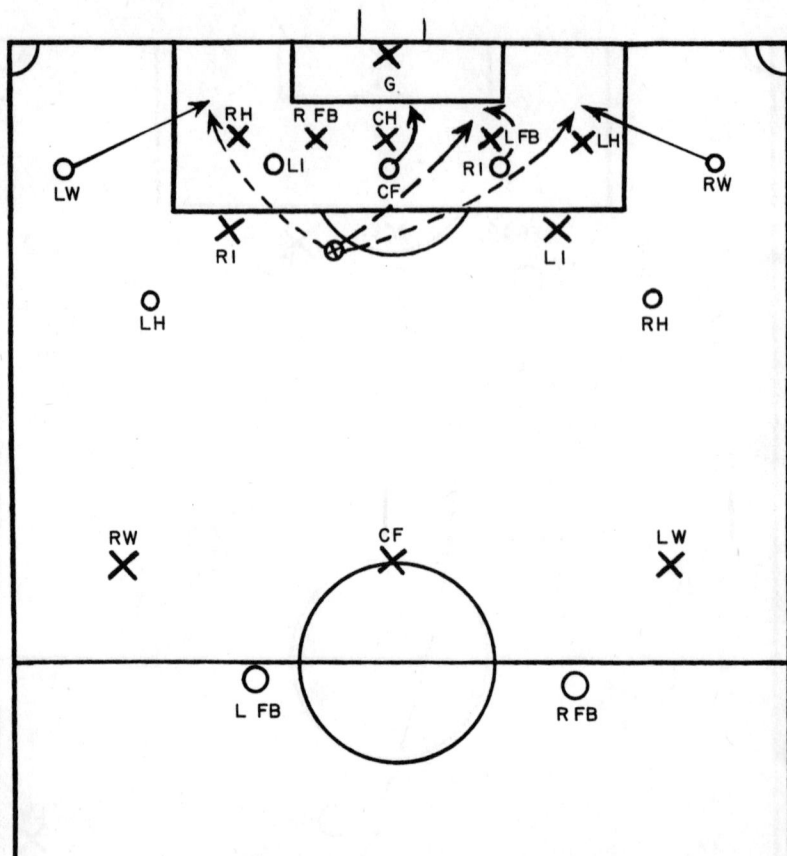

DIAGRAM 49   DIRECT FREE KICK SITUATION WHEN
FREE KICK IS TAKEN JUST OUTSIDE OF
PENALTY BOX IN THE OFFENSIVE END
OF THE FIELD

*With kick just outside of penalty box in the offensive end of the field the possi-
bilities are a direct kick at the goal or a lob pass over the heads of the defense
for the wing forwards to drive in for a goal. Another alternative is a ground
pass to an inside who immediately passes back to half taking kick who then
takes a shot at the goal driving in.*

*On ground pass it should be between the center and either inside with one or
the other driving in for the ball. The one who doesn't drive in blocks out his
man to help set up path for ball to get through.*

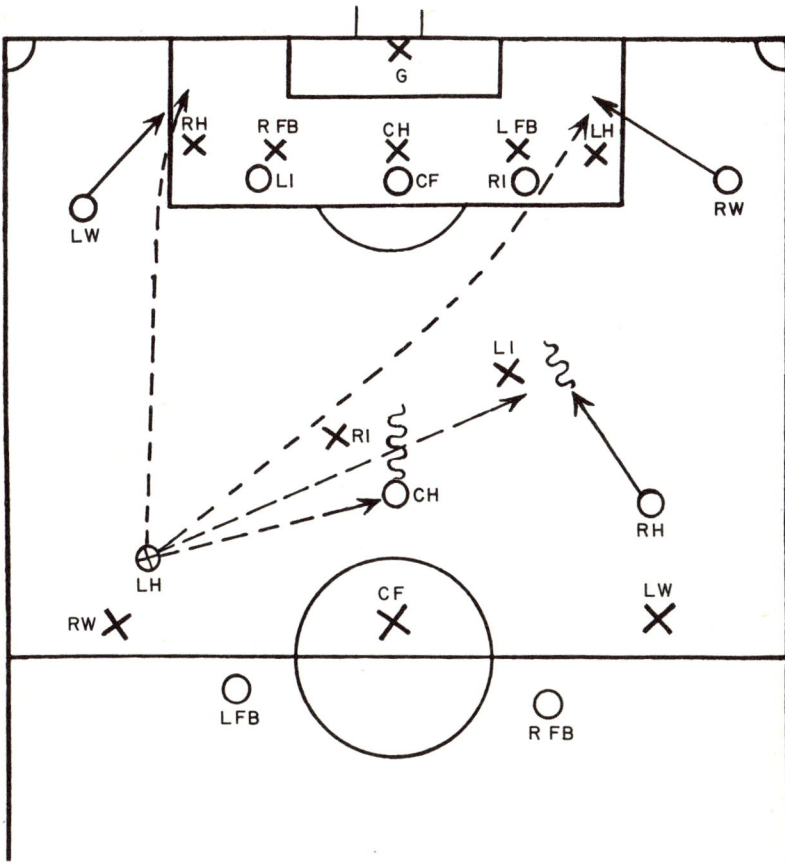

DIAGRAM 50   DIRECT FREE KICK SITUATION—
POSSIBLE PASSES ON FREE KICK IN
OFFENSIVE END OF THE FIELD

Halfback can lob pass to wing driving in or cross pass to wing forward on other side of field for header, pass to either open fellow-halfback for a subsequent dribble in to shoot or ground pass it through the defense in the middle or lob cross pass to opposite wing forward, or to wing forward on the same side of field. The success of any pass to the halfbacks depends entirely on how the opposing inside forwards play. If they play tight as in the diagram, a pass to the halfbacks will not be very effective. However, when the insides play the halfbacks loosely, a pass to one of them will prove effective and open up the defense.

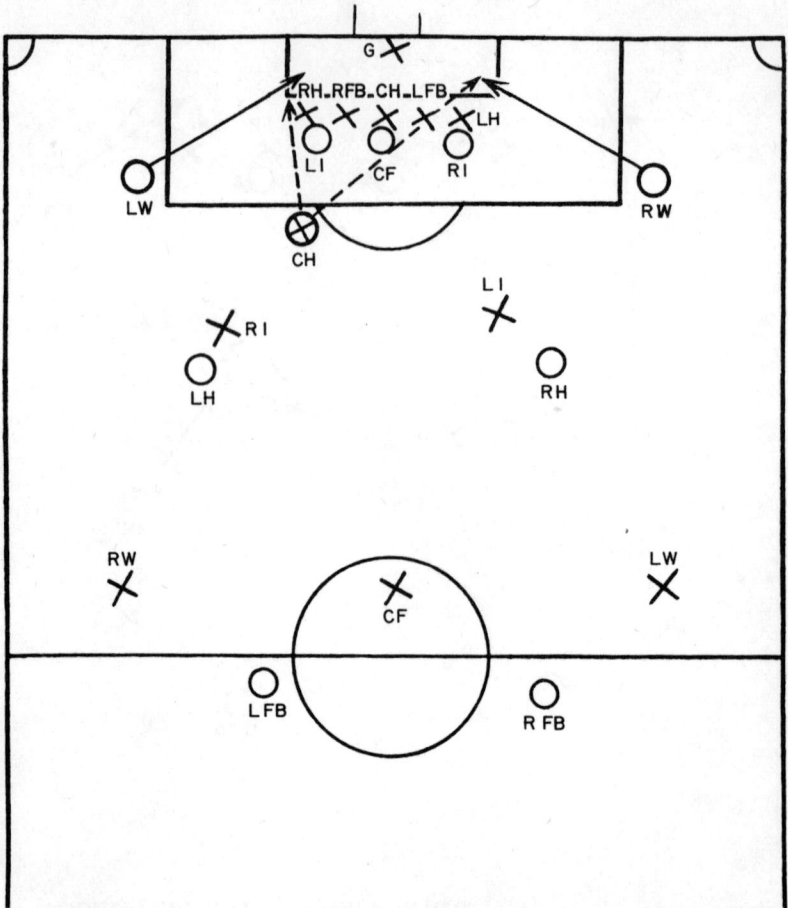

DIAGRAM 51   INDIRECT FREE KICK TAKEN JUST
                   OUTSIDE OF THE OFFENSIVE PENALTY BOX

On indirect free kick just outside of the penalty box, a lob over the heads of the defense to either wing forward or a push pass between the defense, out of the reach of the goalie, for forwards driving in to pick up for a shot is difficult to stop if timed and placed properly. Signals should be given for all these setups.

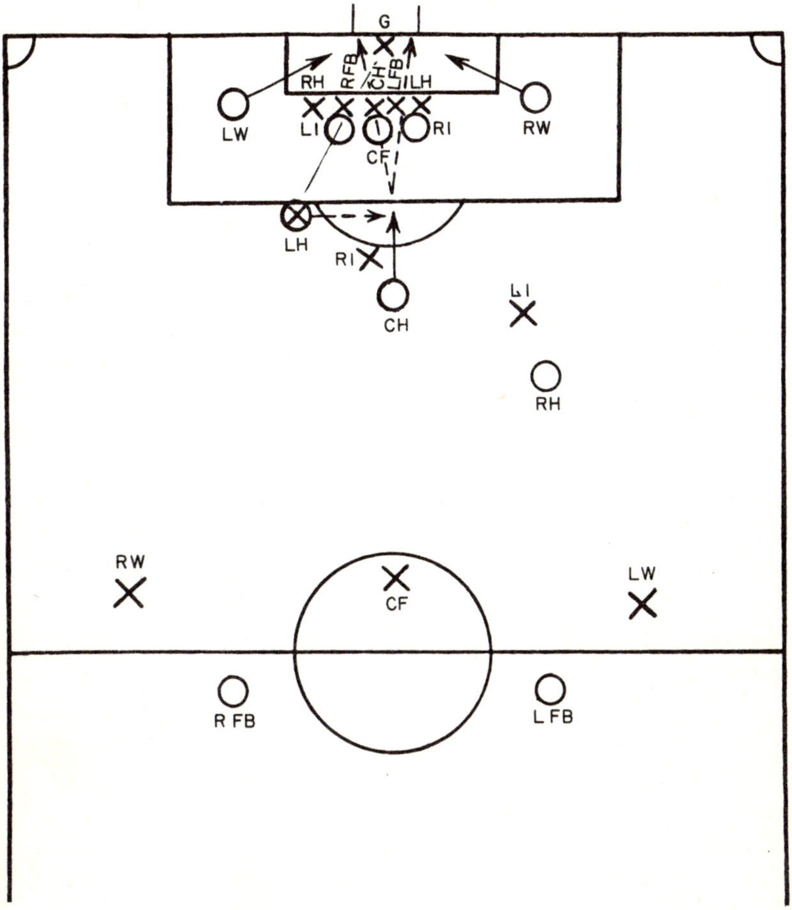

DIAGRAM 52   INDIRECT FREE KICK TAKEN JUST
                    OUTSIDE OF THE OFFENSIVE PENALTY BOX

On indirect free kicks just outside of penalty box a short pass to the side with a man driving in for a direct shot at the goal is very effective. The success or failure of this play obviously depends on how the defensive inside plays the offensive center halfback. If the inside takes a good defensive position, the play will not work. However, if nobody covers the offensive center halfback, then the play as set up in the diagram will be effective.

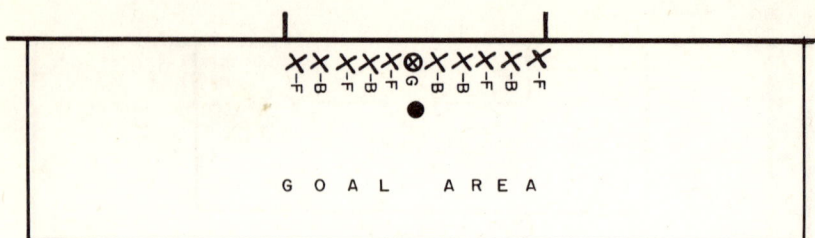

DIAGRAM 53   INDIRECT FREE KICK—INSIDE GOAL AREA
F—FORWARD; B—BACK

In the indirect free kick situation the defense plays in about the same positions as they do in the direct free kick situations with a possibility of being a little bit more conscious of their men, since the kicker cannot score a goal direct with the kick.

There is a possibility of indirect free kicks being taken inside the goal and penalty areas from the spot of the foul. Hence, this presents a decidedly different defensive line-up than any which covers the direct free kicks since all direct free kicks in the goal and penalty areas are taken from the penalty-kick mark. In the indirect free kick situation inside the goal area, where the ten-yard restriction rule is void if the players line up on the goal line between the goalposts, the defensive team lines up on the goal line between the goalposts with the goalie positioning himself about one yard in front of the goal line in the best possible angle position in relation to the position of the ball. The backs and forwards line up alternately on the goal line.

The following diagrams should help a coach in working out any of his own defensive ideas to stop any offensive thrusts from the indirect free kick situations inside the goal and penalty areas.

On the kick the forwards on the defensive team drive out and smother any pass. The backs immediately drive out to pick up their men.

DIAGRAM 54   INDIRECT FREE KICK—INSIDE GOAL AREA
F—FORWARD; B—BACK

If the kick is off to one side of the goal area it is reasonable to play only nine players, including the goalie, or less in the mouth of the goal, thereby leaving

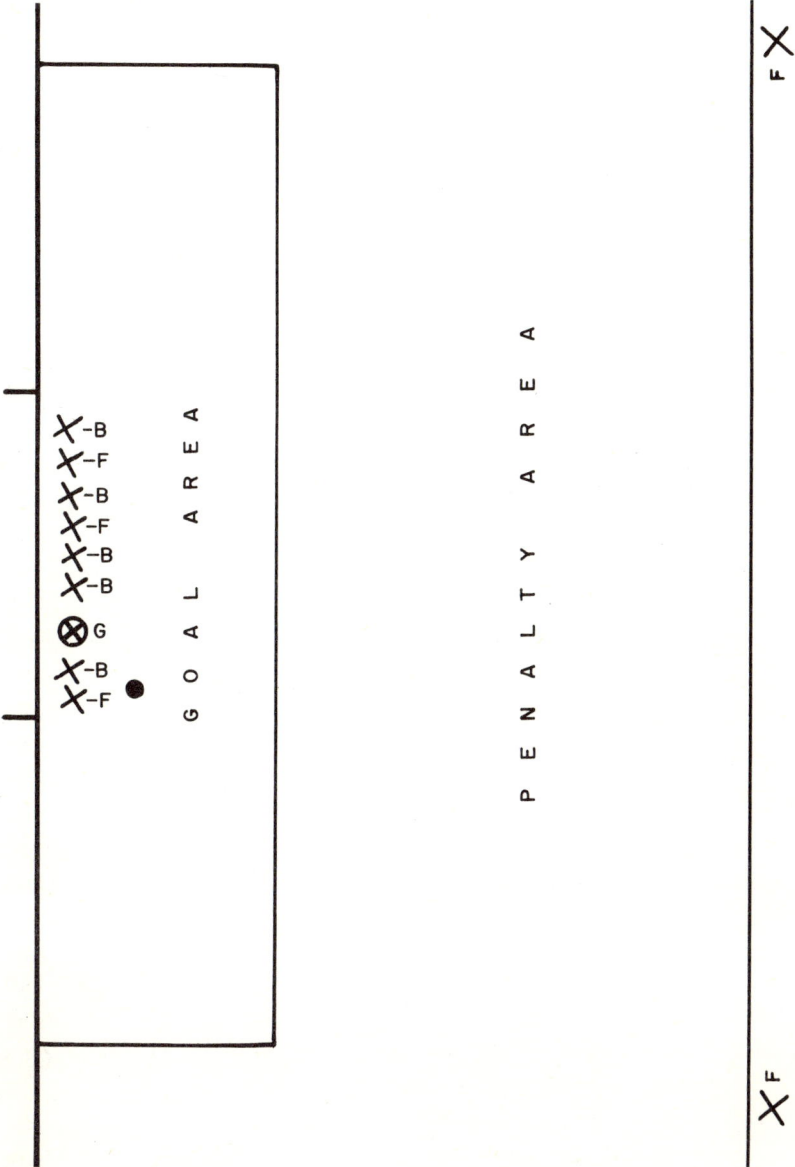

two men up the field ready to take any clearing kicks in order to take the pressure off of the defense and to start an offensive thrust of their own. The nine men on the goal line pack the side on which the kick is being taken and more loosely on the side away from the kicker.

DIAGRAM 55   INDIRECT FREE KICK—PLAY POSSIBILITIES
WHEN TAKEN INSIDE THE PENALTY BOX IN
THE OFFENSIVE END OF THE FIELD

It is rather foolish to kick directly into any packed line set up in the goal. The sensible move is to pass off to a teammate to draw the defense out and make a play on the ball before a successful block by the opponent can be made. The man receiving the pass has many options, such as to kick directly at the goal, to lob a pass to a wing over the heads of the defense, push a pass on the ground between the defense to a man followed by a shot, or a pass to a halfback to open the defense wider followed by a lob cross pass to the wing behind the defense or a direct shot or push pass.

The kicker passes to the right inside who in turn can: 1. lob to either wing forward, 2. push pass through defense to kicker for drive-in shot at goal, 3. pass to one of the halfbacks—halfbacks are usually open and in good position to drive in for shot—lob to wing forwards or push a pass in between the defense, 4. take shot at the goal.

DIAGRAM 56   TOUCH LINE KICKS

Kicks in the offensive end of the field can be placed to any one of the spots indicated by the arrows. All are spot-lead lob passes with the possible exception of the pass to the center halfback which might be on the ground.

Kicks taken down in the defensive end of the field should not be crossed but kicked for distance, as well as accuracy, to a spot for the center, inside or wing on the same side of the field.

Area 1   Touch line kicks taken in this area should be: 1. played the same as corner kick and, 2. kicked by the wing forward.

Area 2   Touch line kicks in this area should be: 1. played the same as a di-

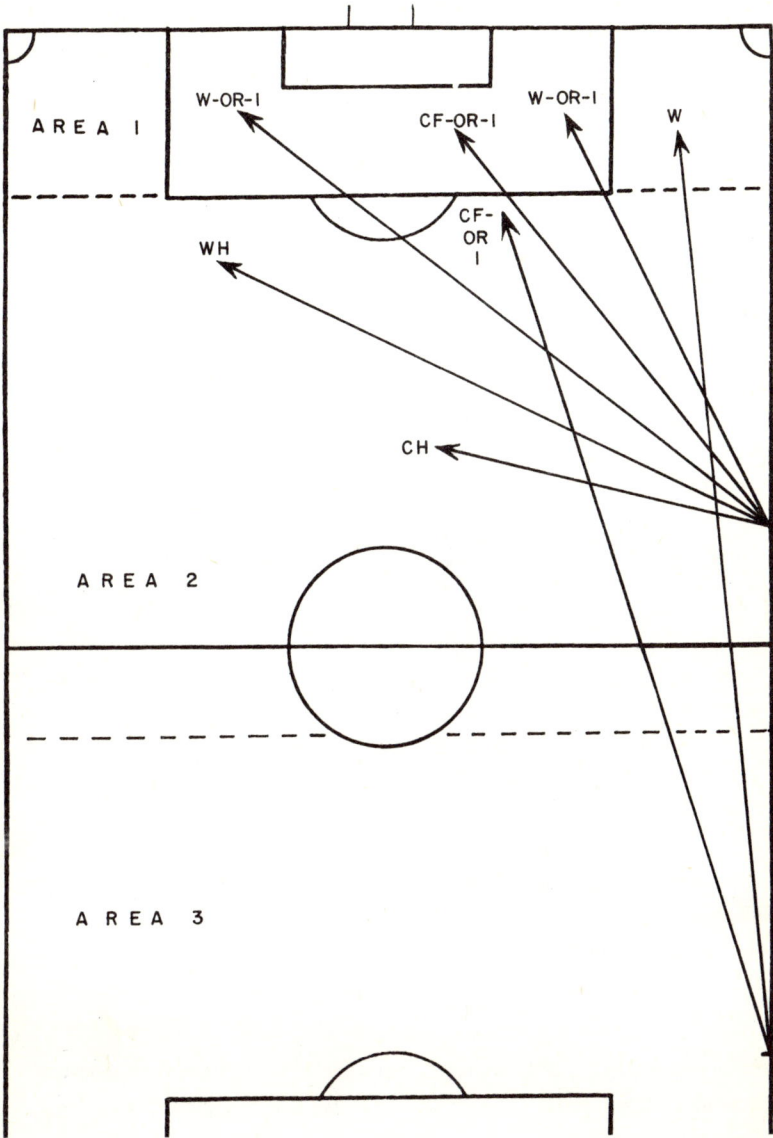

rect free kick and, 2. wing halfbacks take kick beyond the center of field—fullbacks take kick up to center of field.

Area 3   Touch line kicks in this area should be: 1. kicked for distance to forwards on the same side of the field, 2. never cross and, 3. fullbacks take kicks.

VII

Daily Practice Plan, Conditioning Program and Drills

TWO DISTINCT PHASES OF SEASON'S
DAILY PRACTICE PLAN AND CONDITIONING

Every coach, and justifiably so, has his own ideas on what he considers a good practice plan and conditioning program. However, no matter what the plan, it must be so set up that adequate time is given for every phase of the game to be developed in a way to create and sustain interest. This part of the book is written with the hope of making the reader realize how important and how easy it is for the coach to take the field with a well-planned and well-organized practice program. Further, it is hoped to make the reader realize how much more interesting and worthwhile the daily practice sessions can be for the coach and the player when sessions are planned with definite objectives in mind.

180

The season's practice sessions can be divided into two phases. The first phase starts when the boys report in the fall for practice, and winds up with the first game. The second phase starts with the first practice session following the first game and ends with the last practice session of the season.

The first phase depends entirely on the coach to create and maintain interest, whereas, in the second, the coach has the strong support of game competition to keep interest high. The first phase emphasizes conditioning, sizing up, putting round pegs into round holes, weeding out, teaching fundamentals and working on the basic offensive and defensive patterns. The conditioning program should be gradual rather than vigorous. Running is a good conditioner; hence, fundamental drills, such as dribbling and passing while running up and down the field, is good early-season work.

Developing stamina and endurance is a must in order to play the game of soccer well, and more important, to avoid injuries. Besides running, it is important that a set of exercises be used. During the first phase, about ten minutes of each practice session should be set aside for exercises, while during the second phase this time can be cut in half. These exercises should be supplemented by two or three laps around the field at the end of each session. The exercise phase of the program must be well organized and done with plenty of zip. A well-organized and well-planned exercise period can serve to lift the standards, spirit and morale of the practice sessions to a high pitch; on the other hand, if poorly planned and done lethargically, it can do much harm to the sessions. A sound conditioning period should include exercises that will strengthen the ankles, knees, stomach, chest muscles, and increase flexibility of the trunk muscles. The exercises should be few in number and simple, rather than in great quantities and complex, thereby saving time and offering a reasonable guarantee of fulfilling the purpose of each exercise, as the boys are more apt to learn a few correctly.

EXERCISES

The following is a set of exercises which can be used the whole year, with the amount of time allotted for each, at each practice session, being the only changeable factor.

In planning a daily exercise program, the coach should use his own judgment as to the length of time, and make sure that at least one exercise is selected from each of the following groups:

Warm up: 1, 2, 3

Legs: 4, 6, 7, 8, 9, 10, 11, 12, 13, 14, 15, 16

Trunk: 2, 3, 5, 8, 11, 12, 17, 18

1. Starting position—standing, feet together. Warm up with arm-swinging exercise. Swing arms out to side and up over head. Clap hands over head. Combine this with feet jumping apart. Return to starting position.

2. Starting position—standing, feet together. Jump feet apart, bend trunk forward and down, swing extended arms through legs as far back as you can and return.

3. Starting position—standing, feet together. Run in place, bringing knees high up to chest. Start slowly and increase speed.

4. Starting position—standing, legs in stride (feet spread wide apart) position. On 1, bend knee of right leg deep and rest buttocks on heel of right foot. Keep left leg fully extended to side. On 2, return to starting position. On 3, same as 1 to left side. On 4, return to starting position.

5. Starting position—standing, feet together, hands on hips. Rotate trunk on hips. On 1, bend body forward. On 2, twist body to left. On 3, twist and bend trunk back at hips. On 4, twist trunk to right. On 5, back to starting position.

6. Starting position—standing erect, heels together, toes pointed slightly outward, hands on hips. On 1, deep-knee bend, trunk straight. On 2, return to starting position.

7. Starting position—same as 6. On 1, deep-knee bend, hands on ground between legs. On 2, legs thrown backward to front leaning rest position. On 3, back to deep-knee bend position. On 4, back to starting position.

8. Starting position—supine (lying on back), arms at sides. On 1, come up to sitting position. On 2, keep knees stiff, reach out and grab feet. On 3, return to starting position.

9. Starting position—front leaning rest position (weight borne by hands, arms extended, and toes, stomach toward ground). Bounce in place.

10. Starting position—front leaning rest position. On 1, bounce and separate arms and feet as far as possible. On 2, return to starting position.

11. Starting position—back leaning rest (weight borne by hands and heels of feet, back to ground). Raise hips as high as possible and return.

12. Starting position—front leaning rest position. Raise hips as high as possible and return.

13. Starting position—lie on right side. Left leg whipping: from hip swing leg as far forward and backward as possible.

14. Starting position—lie on left side. Right leg whipping: from hip swing leg as far forward and backward as possible.

15. Starting position—front leaning rest position. Leg pumping: bring right knee up to chest and back very fast, bring left knee up to chest and back very fast.

16. Starting position—kneeling position, arms overhead. On 1, bend backwards from knees. On 2, back to starting position.

17. Starting position—prone (lying on ground face down), with arms fully extended over head. On 1, raise arms and legs off ground as high as possible. On 2, return to starting position.

18. Starting position—supine, hands on back of head. On 1, raise trunk and bring left leg up toward chest. Twist trunk and touch left knee with elbow of right arm. On 2, return to starting position. On 3, same as 1, only use right leg and left arm. On 4, return to starting position.

TEACHING FUNDAMENTALS AND
BASIC TEAM PATTERNS

There are two schools of thought on how to teach fundamentals. One is of the feeling that the boys learn more through scrimmaging, while the other feels that a definite time should be set aside each day to develop perfection through repetition. I happen to be of the feeling that the emphasis should be on drill work under supervision with constant repetition, especially with the beginners. In basketball, for example, a boy practices his foul shots every day by repetition until the mechanics of the shot are well grooved and mechanically perfect. All basketball coaches will agree that daily practice and drilling on this fundamental, as well as others, is a must, so that when a boy meets the situation in a game the percentages are all in his favor. I feel the same way regarding the teaching of soccer fundamentals. There must, of course, be a chance for a boy to put these fundamentals to use in scrimmage every day, but the emphasis in teaching fundamentals must be through drill work.

Scrimmages offer the boys the opportunity to put into use their fundamentals, but more important to learn how to play together in their basic offensive and defensive patterns. Position play must always be emphasized while scrimmaging.

Wise use of available time is important. All players do not show up on the field at the same time; many of them get out on the field a good half hour before the practice session is scheduled to start. This is an excellent time to work with individuals, and to get to know each other a little bit better. It is also a wonderful chance for boys to work on their own particular weaknesses. It is a great opportunity to contact each boy from time to time and make sure that each is headed in the right direction, and understands the patterns of the team play and of his own particular position. At this time a coach can iron out many misunderstandings merely by talking with a player or possibly players who he has a feeling are dissatisfied for one reason or another. A timely pat on the back, a word of encouragement, and some sound advice often gets a boy over the hump and on his way.

Many coaches use the buddy system in teaching fundamentals, and in some cases, not all, it has proved to be very successful. In the buddy system two boys pair up and work on their fundamentals together. For example, in heading, one buddy can throw the ball while the other heads. They can work on heading for accuracy, forward, sideward, and backward. They can head for distance, head to lob over an onrushing opponent and drive around to get control of the ball. All the fundamentals can be worked on this way before and during practice if the coach so desires. It certainly creates a fine feeling of interest, pride and concern in each other's progress.

After the exercises the coach can follow any procedure he feels is best; however, the standard procedure seems to be for the coach to explain and demonstrate the fundamentals to be worked on for the day, as well as simple drills emphasizing a definite part of the game. The offense as well as the defense, should be broken down into parts and the parts worked on as drills. On offense, simply having two offensive men take the ball around one defensive man requires the use of many fundamentals. For the offense it emphasizes drawing the defensive man; passing off with a push pass on the ground; and cutting around and behind the defensive man for a repass. This is the simple triangle play which is often used. For the defense it means developing the skill or knack of positioning oneself in the proper position to intercept the pass and get the ball. Again the amount of time spent on each will have to be left entirely up to the coach's judgment. As a matter of fact, although many times a coach sets aside so much time for one particular drill, he might find it wise in maintaining interest to cut the time short and move on to another phase of the game.

When introducing drills it is important that the boys know exactly what is trying to be accomplished and how it fits into the whole picture. It is discouraging sometimes to hear boys say, near the end of the season, that they are just beginning to understand what you, as a coach, want them to do. Demonstrate, talk and use a blackboard in explaining the drills, since some boys, who might not be able to understand an explanation one way, can pick it up easily another. The coach must keep pounding it home.

PRACTICE SESSIONS—First Phase

During the first phase of the practice sessions the basic offensive and defensive patterns must be explained and worked on tenaciously. At the beginning of the season it is wise to have a few skull sessions in the early evening to discuss this feature of the game so that time can be saved during the practice sessions for the actual physical workouts. Further, at a discussion period the boys are more apt to ask questions, and the coach, undoubtedly, will cover the ground more thoroughly. A discussion period will certainly create interest through a better understanding of the game and oftentimes create good feeling and respect between the coach and the players.

It is wise to include in every practice session a scrimmage, and during the scrimmage use the policy of stopping play to point out omissions and commissions whenever either are evident. This whole method of teaching can be very helpful if used along with the drill work. Again, the amount of time the coach allows for the scrimmages will depend a good deal on what he thinks the players need, based on their performances during practice, and once the season opens, based on their game performances. Although I have emphasized the importance of drill work in teaching fundamentals, the coach must also realize that scrimmaging is a must in a team's training program. Both phases are important.

It is important in any practice session to keep the boys eagerly working at top speed and interested enough so that they will hesitatingly leave the field at the end of the session.

During the first phase of the daily practice and conditioning schedule, the following must be covered:

1. Conditioning
2. Fundamentals

3. Drills on special setups, including indirect and direct free kicks, penalty kicks, corner kicks, goal kicks, touch line kicks, opening kick-off plays, line-ups, etc.
4. Basic offensive and defensive patterns
5. Scrimmaging

PRACTICE SESSIONS—Second Phase

The second phase of the season's practice sessions differs from the first in that competition with other schools is now a part of the picture, which, per se, makes the boys realize that games are won by the amount of work accomplished in practice during the week. Practice sessions planned around games seem to have a little bit more glamour and make a little bit more sense to the boys than merely practicing for a spell without any immediate objective in sight. Games are the showcase, and boys inherently want to look good when on display. Because of this, and because weaknesses are so obvious in games, it doesn't take much to sell the boys on why they have to work before they can expect to come up with good game performances.

After every game a coach should wisely go over every detail of the game both individual and team, explain the reasons why, and then set out to correct weaknesses. Through competition the boys gain experience and confidence and with it they begin to do the things in games they have practiced so earnestly for many weeks. With this, the coach begins to glamorize the basic offensive and defensive patterns. He adds switching and decoy combinations. He gives the boys more freedom in their play, and they begin to feel the real impact of team play. All this makes the practice sessions more interesting and spirited.

DRILLS

Drills do not have to be complex to be effective; make them simple and make them serve a definite purpose, and, whenever possible, introduce into them the element of competition.

FIGURE 2   **A-LINE FORMATION**

Two lines—Line 1 and Line 2 always set up as in the following diagram:

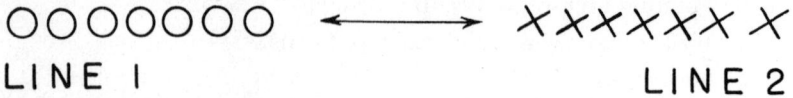

O O O O O O O   ⟵⟶   X X X X X X X

LINE 1   **LINE 2**

In going through the drill the number one man in both lines should always go to the end of the opposite line after going through the exercise.

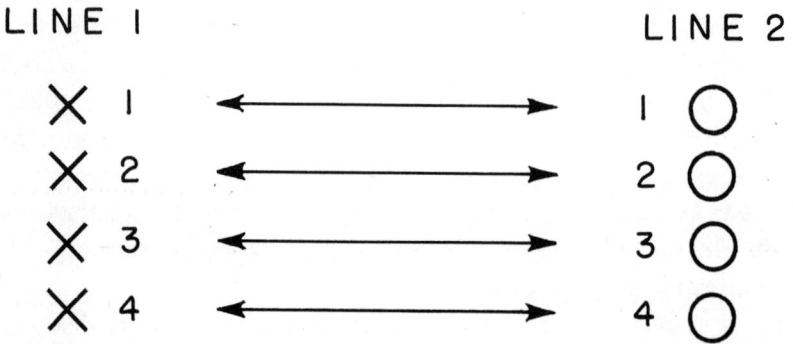

LINE 1   **LINE 2**

X 1   ⟵⟶   1 O
X 2   ⟵⟶   2 O
X 3   ⟵⟶   3 O
X 4   ⟵⟶   4 O

FIGURE 3   **B-LINE FORMATION**

Two lines—Line 1 and Line 2.
    X_1 in Line 1 faces O_1 in Line 2;
    X_2 in Line 1 faces O_2 in Line 2; etc.

X X X X X X X X ⟶

FIGURE 4   **C-LINE FORMATION**

Players merely line up in a straight line one man in back of the other.

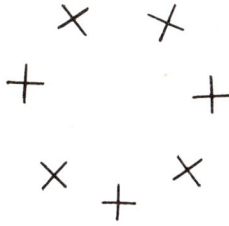

FIGURE 5 CIRCLE FORMATION

START FINISH

FIGURE 6 ZIGZAG FORMATION

Can be used in setting up obstacle races employing the dribble or in passing drills.

Make sure every boy knows the purpose of each drill and the exact mechanics of each move. Have the boys walk through the drills first, and, as they improve, have them increase their speed. In watching boys practice fundamentals, make sure you allow for individual differences.

In drill work the fewer the numbers in each squad and the more balls available, and in use, the more work done.

In setting up drills to teach fundamentals, the following formations are the simplest and the most common:

Kicking

A practice widely used in teaching boys to kick with their instep is to start them off by using sneakers rather than regular soccer shoes. The use of sneakers discourages the use of the toe. A ball can be controlled and, hence, kicked more accurately with the instep than the toe. In all kicking drills the players should attempt to kick for accuracy to spots and to men. Kicks should be short at first; length of kicks should be increased as the players improve.

Drills

A—Use A formation, first man in line one can do one of the
following: (in all these kicks the kicker should kick to a
spot)

1. Roll the ball to the first man in line 2 who kicks without
   trapping.
2. Bounce the ball to the first man in line 2 who half-volley
   kicks.
3. High lob the ball to the first man in line 2 who uses clearance volley kick. After throwing the ball the thrower should
   drive in toward the kicker.

B—Use B-line formation. Players kicking ball back and forth
with simple instep kick to a specific man in the opposite
line. This setup can be used to practice all kicks.

Accuracy in kicking comes first, followed by kicking for distance. Perfection of the clearance volley kick is a must for the fullbacks, for it is definitely associated with the fullbacks. Fullbacks
should practice this kick to attain some degree of accuracy in hitting a spot for the wing forwards or center forward to pick up and
get control of the ball. For the halfbacks, in addition to the above,
simple drills should be set up to develop accuracy in feeding the
forwards and to spots inside the penalty box out of the reach of the
goalie. The halfbacks should also work on dribbling in and shooting from about the front line of the penalty box.

The wing forwards should put the emphasis on developing a
good cross, usually a pivot kick. Have the wing forwards dribble
down the side of the field and cross to a spot. Since the wing forwards must develop a good shot, drills should be worked out so
that they can dribble in and shoot. A simple combination drill
with the inside forward push-passing the ball behind the defense
to the wing forward, who traps and shoots, or shoots without trapping, is used very often in a game, and is a worthwhile drill for the
wing forward in developing a shot. Kicking to circles on the field
or marks on the field makes for a good deal of sustained interest.

For the forwards, drills set up to develop shots should be used every day, with the first-string goalie in the nets most of the time.

Drills for Inside and Center Forwards

Use C-line formation

1. Have inside and center forwards dribble in on the right side of the goal and shoot with the right foot.
2. Same players dribble in from the left side and shoot with the left foot.
3. Players dribble down middle, hit with either foot. Obstacles can be used in these drills, for example, dribbling and snaking around two or three stakes or men before shooting.

In this set of drills use the A-line formation with the number 1 line to one side of and behind the goalpost and the number 2 line on the front line of penalty box in front of the mouth of the goal.

4. First man in line 1 rolls the ball on the ground to the first man in line 2 who drives in to meet the ball and shoots without trapping. Alternate shooting first with the right foot and then with the left.
5. Bounce ball out—half-volley kick—strong shot.
6. High bounce—full volley kick—will be a stab at the ball with knee bent, force coming from extension of knee.
7. Pull number 1 line to the right side of penalty box and about twelve yards from goal line. Follow same procedure as in 4, 5, and 6. In this drill the players can first trap and shoot or shoot without trapping.
8. Pull number 1 line to the left side of penalty box and about twelve yards from goal line. Follow same procedure as in 7.
9. Pull number 1 line out to just beyond front of penalty box facing goal, number 2 line sets up around spot-kick mark. Follow same drills as in 4, 5 and 6 with players in number 2 line receiving ball with back to goal, pivoting and kicking the ball at goal. It will be a trap and pivot shot or merely a pivot shot. These shots should be and will be hit to the corners of the goal.

Trapping

Simplest drills are set up using B-line formation. It will save time in the beginning if the ball is thrown by one player at another to practice specific traps, such as chest, stomach, sole of foot, inside of foot, inside of leg, outside of foot.

1. Use B-line formation. Players kick, with accuracy, to a man in the opposite line who traps, sets up and kicks back to a specific man in the opposite line.

2. Use circle formation. Advisable to use with the coach or a veteran player in the middle of the circle throwing the ball to each boy in turn and constructively criticizing.

Dribbling

Relays should be set up using the A-line, or the circle, or zig-zag formations.

1. Simple relay using A-line formation with first man in line 1 dribbling ball to first man in line 2 who shuttles back, etc. Dribbler after finishing always goes to end of line he just dribbled to.

2. For variation of 1. Separate men about fifteen feet apart and have last man in line 1 snake his way down around men in his line and dribble down to last man in line 2 who snakes his way around men in his line, etc. After finishing exercise player goes to head of opposite line.

3. Use circle formation:

   a. Boys about ten feet apart, not more than six in a circle. First man dribbles clockwise completely around the circle and back to original position and passes the ball off to the man to his left who does exactly what the number one man did. This is done until every player in the circle has gone through the drill. The exercise should then be done with players going counter-clockwise.

   b. Same formation—number one man snakes his way around men in circle and passes off to player lined up to his left. Exercise is done first clockwise then counter-clockwise.

c. Use zigzag formation. Last man in line snakes his way around the men in line from one end to the other and dribbles to a spot about thirty yards beyond his own line and back to give the ball to the last man in his line. After he passes off he goes to the front of the line. The race ends when all the boys in the line have gone through the drill.

d. Dribble for speed—outside of foot.
Use A-line formation—Relay race.
Boys in line 1 merely dribble the length of the field to the first man in line 2, who dribbles the ball back to the first man in line 1, etc. Emphasis should be on dribbling the ball with the outside of the foot in a straight line for speed.

e. A valuable drill combining passing, trapping, and dribbling is for two boys to dribble and pass the ball together down the length of the field and back.

It is wise occasionally to set up dribbling drills which will present the psychological effect of a defensive man right behind the dribbler. To set up a situation use the two-on-one situation. The defensive man should do his job according to the rule of thumb, but the pass receiver instead of repassing dribbles the ball down the field with the defensive man chasing him. If the defensive man annoys the dribbler enough so that he cannot get a shot or a pass-off, the dribbler should stop, pivot, pass back to his teammate and cut behind the defense to receive a repass.

Passing

Use both A- and B-line formations and circle formation to practice passing.

Accuracy in passing can be developed by using markers and passing while dribbling in combination with a teammate. Emphasize in all passing the lead so that the receiver can drive to the ball to pick it up. Any combination drill will offer the opportunity to improve passing skill.

Lob Inside-of-the-Foot Pass

Use A-line formation.

First man in the line 1 throws the ball in the air to the first man in line 2 who lobs the ball to a spot with the inside of the foot over the head of the man driving in.

Flick Pass

Two men dribble the ball down the field about ten feet apart, flick passing the ball to each other. Dribbling down and back will offer each boy the opportunity of practice with both the right and the left foot.

Goalie

In working and setting up drills to develop the goalie's skills, the coach should first explain each skill carefully and then throw or roll the ball into the mouth of the goal to necessitate the use of the skill discussed. In throwing the ball it will save time and the mechanics of one particular skill can be concentrated on and discussed carefully as the work is going on. When the coach is sure that the goalies understand the mechanics of each skill and can perform them reasonably well, balls should be kicked toward goal from every conceivable angle. The goalie should be in the goal on every free kick drill situation and all drills that include the ball actually being shot at the mouth of the goal. Both the goalie and the boy who is assigned to shoot the penalty kick should set aside a time each day to work on their specialty.

Drills to Develop Team Efforts:

1. Two-on-one
   Two defensive men try to get by one defensive man by the use of the draw, pass-off, cut and repass.
2. Three-on-one
   Same principles involved as in two-on-one, i.e., draw, pass-off, and cut. Try to make defensive man commit himself.

3. Wings dribble down the side of the field, cross to inside and wing on the opposite side of the field driving in. Ball should be placed inside of the penalty box, in front of the far goalpost out of the reach of the goalie.

4. Set up all free kick situations as drills including direct and indirect free kicks, touch line kick, goal kick, corner kick and spot penalty kick.

5. Switching drills, such as, wing driving into the inside position with the inside automatically going out to the wing. Use switching play patterns as drills.

6. Switching drills on defense should be worked in. All plays should be practiced and set up as drills, including opening kick-off plays and decoy plays.

   Obviously the more times a play or setup is repeated, the better the chance of successfully handling the situation when it comes up in a game.

As a slight divergence from the regular practice routine, six-man soccer and keep-away games can be used. Most games are either too complex, or the players have to be jugglers to really derive any satisfaction from them. Six-man soccer opens the field and because of it the players learn the importance of lead kicks to spots and open men and the value of position play. In the keep-away game, which can be played on half the field, the boys use every fundamental they know and realize the importance of accurate passing, and also the importance of positioning themselves on the field for a pass and a repass. One other method which can be of some help, if only in a psychological way, is playing games using only the weak foot. I would certainly use it occasionally as a wise divergent from the regular routine with the hope of driving home a point.

Drills, although not a substitute for game experience, do have something in common with it, in that both offer the players the opportunity of meeting a situation often enough to develop confidence and know-how.

VIII

Glossary

ANTICIPATION—A seventh sense developed by a soccer player which usually finds him in the right place at the right time, positioning himself almost as if by intuition. This comes through study and experience and intelligent observation of the opponents. It is more than mere guessing; it is the sense of knowing what the opponent is going to do before he does it.

BACK-UP—A term used on defense when one defensive player falls in behind another defensive player to back up his moves.

CLEARING KICK—A clearing kick or clear is a kick made by a player which usually sends the ball out of danger from his own end of the field toward and sometimes into the opponent's end of the field for a teammate to pick up and start an offensive thrust.

COMBINATION—Any setup or play involving two or more players on the same team designed to outwit the opponents.

CORNER KICK—A direct free kick taken from a corner of the field, Awarded to the opponents of team A when a player on team A last touches the ball before it goes out of bounds over team A's own goal line. It is kicked from the corner of the field nearest the spot where the ball went over the goal line.

CROSS—A ball kicked from one side of the field to the other. A kick most commonly associated with the wing forwards. When the wing forwards do cross the ball, it is a kick across the field to a spot out of the reach of the goalie in front of the far goalpost, with the idea of setting it up for the wing forward and inside on the opposite side of the field to drive in and shoot at the goal.

DECOY PLAY OR MOVE—A play or move made by a player to draw an opponent away from a spot and open up a scoring lane or spot for a teammate to drive into for a pass and possible shot at the goal.

DEFENSIVE END OF THE FIELD

YOUR END OF THE FIELD—That half of the field toward which your opponents are driving to score a goal. The end you are guarding.

DIRECT FREE KICK—A free kick from which a goal can be scored directly by the kicker. Usually any personal foul.

DRAW—The act which pulls an opponent to you. This is usually done when a player dribbles to pull a man to him and away from a teammate which will open or free the teammate for a pass. This is considered the basic pattern of the short passing game but should be used whenever the situation presents itself, especially when there are two offensive men faced with only one defensive man. The act of drawing a man to you will open up many combination possibilities.

FIRST-TIME KICK—Kicking a ball without trapping it.

GOAL KICK—An indirect free kick awarded to team A when the opponents kick the ball out of play over team A's goal line. The ball is kicked from the front corner of the goal area on the side of the goal where the ball was kicked out over the goal line. To be put into play the ball must be kicked forward in any direction and beyond the boundaries of the penalty box.

GOAL LINE—The boundary lines at the ends of the field.

HORIZONTAL AXIS OF THE BALL—The axis of the ball which is parallel to the ground.

INDIRECT FREE KICK—A free kick from which a goal cannot be scored directly by the kicker. The ball must be touched first by another player. Usually any technical foul, such as, ball going out of bounds.

INSIDE OF FOOT—All that part of the foot on the big toe side from the ankle down.

INSTEP—That part of the foot roughly along the lace of the shoe.

KICK TO A SPOT—Kicking a ball to a logical open or uncovered spot on the field where a teammate can expect the ball to be kicked and can drive in to pick it up.

LEAD PASS—A pass made ahead of the intended receiver so that he can pick it up and drive on without reducing his speed.

LOFT OR LOB—A high soft kick, usually a kick over the heads of the defense.

OFFENSIVE END OF THE FIELD

OPPONENT'S END OF THE FIELD—That half of the field toward which your team is driving to score a goal. The end of the field the opponents are guarding.

OFF-SIDE—Basic rules concerning off-side are:

    a. There must be two opposing players between an offensive player and the opponent's goal unless an opponent or the player himself last touched it. (THE GOALIE IS CONSIDERED A PLAYER).

    b. A player cannot be off-side in his own half of the field.

    c. A player cannot be off-side on:

        (1) a goal kick.

        (2) a corner kick.

        (3) a dropped ball

        (4) if player is behind the ball when it is last played.

    (Check rule book for special situations.)

ON-SIDE—Check off-side.

PENALTY BOX—An area eight yards by forty-four yards directly in front of the mouth of the goal. The goalie can use his hands only in this area.

RIDING A BALL OR CUSHIONING A BALL—A way of reducing the speed of a ball coming at a player, and bringing it under control, by using the head, body or feet. Done by giving at the part of body where the ball hits at the time of impact.

SAVE—A stop, by the goalie, of a shot at the goal by one of the opponents.

SPOT KICK OR

PENALTY KICK—A direct free kick from a spot twelve yards out from the mouth of the goal awarded to a team when an opposing player commits a personal foul inside his penalty box.

SWITCH—When a player assumes the position on the field ordinarily covered by another player and in turn the other player assumes his position. It is natural to assume that two or more players are usually involved in a switch, i.e., if A switches to B's position, B will automatically switch to A's position on the field.

TOUCH LINE—The boundary lines on the side of the field. Often called the sidelines.

TOUCH LINE KICK—A free kick from the touch line, kicked from the spot where the ball left the playing field. The kick is awarded to the opponents of the player who last touched it before it went out of bounds. This is an indirect free kick.

VERTICAL AXIS OF THE BALL—The axis of the ball which is perpendicular to the ground.

Index